RAILWAYS
IN THE YEARS OF PRE-EMINENCE
1905–1919

Railways of the World in Color

RAILWAYS

IN THE YEARS OF PRE-EMINENCE

1905–1919

by
O. S. NOCK

Illustrated by
CLIFFORD and WENDY MEADWAY

THE MACMILLAN COMPANY

Library of Congress Catalog Card Number: 76–152282

First American Edition 1971
First published in Great Britain in 1971 by the
Blandford Press Ltd, London

THE MACMILLAN COMPANY
866 Third Avenue, New York, NY 10022

Printed in Great Britain
Color section printed in Holland

PREFACE

In the first volume of this series of books having the general title of 'Railways of the World in Colour', that dealing with *Railways at the Turn of the Century 1895–1905*, I referred in the Preface to the difficulty experienced in tracing the colours of locomotives, carriages, and equipment—not only in remote parts of the world, but in countries where one might have expected the documentation to be extensive. That difficulty has not diminished as the artists and author have progressed to successive volumes. This, the third in the new series, has had to be completed with references to some countries still entirely lacking. It is nevertheless the experience of most authors of descriptive and historical works that one has only got to get a book into print before readers write in to provide additional and important information which lay hitherto concealed, and apparently beyond the reach of so-called 'official' sources. This has occurred since the publication of volume two, covering the years of the *Zenith of Steam 1920–40*, but after the present volume was completely proofed, and 'ready to run', as the term goes.

When this series is complete we hope to fill in a few of the gaps in the world coverage that have been so far inevitable, even though it will mean overlapping the chronological periods allocated to each of the remaining volumes. There is indeed some slight overlapping in the present one, as indicated in the final sentences of the introduction. In the meantime our researches continue. While the literature of railways is immense it is important to appreciate that a high proportion of it is retrospective. Prior to the year 1896, when *Moore's Monthly Magazine* first appeared as the forerunner of the *Locomotive, Carriage and Wagon Review*, and July 1897 when *The Railway Magazine* was inaugurated, the only contemporary reporting of railway matters concerned finance, and the purely technical aspects of railway engineering. In *The Locomotive*, particularly, many superb photographs taken in earlier days began to come to light, but the references to *colour* were so scanty as to be almost negligible.

Furthermore, photographs can be definitely misleading, especially the fine official pictures of locomotives built by some of the leading private manufacturers. An example exists even in the period covered by this book. Just at the close of the first World War the Tyneside firm of Hawthorn, Leslie & Co. Ltd. built some new 4–6–0s for the Highland Railway. The official builders' photographs showed these engines fully lined out, whereas in fact they went into service in the plain, unlined green then standard on the Highland Railway. Local knowledge, widely appreciated by present day students of locomotive history, in this instance prevented any chance of a 'class' being depicted in a form in which it never ran; but what was possible with a well-known British type might not be so readily possible with locomotives exported far overseas, of which the only photographs available to us are those taken before shipment. But as emphasised in the first volume such hazards merely add to the interest and worthwhileness of the research; and the artists and I are most grateful to an increasing number of pen-friends overseas who have given us most generously of their help.

Brock

Silver Cedars,
High Bannerdown,
Batheaston,
BATH

February 1971.

INTRODUCTION

For a period of about twenty years, roughly from 1905 to 1925, railways were without question the pre-eminent means of transport on land everywhere in the world. In Great Britain, on one special occasion, speed had topped 100 m.p.h.; new branch lines were being developed, and where railways did not previously exist light railways were being constructed to open up rural districts. In Great Britain, as in Europe generally, railways had no serious competition for any journeys beyond urban areas, and even in the large cities the construction of electric underground lines was proving a much more satisfactory alternative to electric tram-cars in the streets. As yet the petrol-driven motor-bus had barely begun to make any impact. On the railways themselves, with few isolated exceptions, the established main lines were operated wholly by steam locomotives.

Only in France and the U.S.A. was the British supremacy in speed of service seriously challenged. In France the Northern Railway was operating some very fast trains, and in the U.S.A. the rival express services working between Philadelphia and Atlantic City had already established a reputation for high speed. There were also some fast services on the level routes radiating from Chicago. In this book, however, we are not primarily concerned with speed. It is the railway scene in this colourful period that is so fascinating, as the differing trends in locomotive design in various parts of the world are studied, and the influences that led to those practices are traced to their origins. At the same time the development of carriages both for ordinary traffic and special duties showed a general seeking after greater comfort and, indeed, luxury on lengthy runs overseas that involved journeys extending over both night and day. The evolution of wagon design also showed the growing appreciation of the need for conveyance of minerals and general merchandise in larger units of load.

In locomotive design, viewing the entire world, the influence of Great Britain remained immensely strong, and in Glasgow the continuing high output of the three factories of the North British Locomotive Company, Hyde Park, Queen's Park, and Atlas, made that city the greatest centre of export trade in locomotives to be found anywhere in the world. Great American firms like Baldwin and the American Locomotive Company, probably had a greater total output, but a high proportion of that output was for the home market. Unlike Britain very few of the American railways designed and built their own locomotives. One could recognize a much greater similarity in the appearance of locomotives on the different railways of America than among the highly individual styles of the British railways in pre-grouping days, and one needs to study technical features in some detail to appreciate some of the special requirements specified by different administrations; whereas in Great Britain the outward and visible differences in styling and finish were often quite startling.

An immediate distinction between British and American locomotives was in the simple matter of size. It is true that the American loading gauge permitted of locomotives being built somewhat taller than in Great Britain, but the enormous length and girth of the boilers was most striking, even in the first decade of the twentieth century. The difference can immediately be traced to the nature of the fuel. In Great Britain the railways were fortunate in being able to obtain unlimited supplies of first-class bituminous coal. Its characteristics varied in different coalfields, and a different technique in firing was needed with the hard coals of South Yorkshire and Nottinghamshire to that with the soft grades of South Wales, which had a very high calorific value. But all these British coals enabled locomotives to be built with relatively small boilers and fireboxes. Although the over-all process of steam raising did not show a high thermal efficiency compared with other forms of power development by heat transfer, the combustion in the fireboxes of British locomotives was a great deal more efficient than was possible with the coals in contemporary use in the U.S.A. and Canada. There, very large boilers with huge firegrates were needed to raise the steam necessary for traction from the poor quality coal.

On the continent of Europe, conditions varied considerably. Many countries had indigenous supplies of coal, but much of it was of a quality far below that mined in Great Britain. Certain railways, notably the Paris, Lyons, and Mediterranean, purchased Welsh coal for their express locomotives, and operated their own fleet of colliers to convey the coal from Cardiff docks to Marseilles. Locomotive coal was also shipped from the Yorkshire coalfields via Immingham docks near Grimsby to the Baltic States and to Russia. The outward physical characteristics of British locomotives were also to be seen in South America. Many of the railways were British-owned, and they purchased their locomotive fuel from South Wales. Welsh

and Scottish coal was also exported to Ireland for railway purposes. Generally speaking oil firing was in its infancy all over the world. Even before the turn of the century the Great Eastern Railway had made a successful introduction of oil firing, on a limited scale, to utilize the waste products of Stratford Works; and this system was applied, with local modifications, again to a limited extent, during the period of a prolonged coal strike in Great Britain in 1912.

Nevertheless, despite the far greater boilers and fireboxes permitted by the American loading gauge haulage problems were growing to such an extent that an orthodox locomotive, however large and heavy, was not powerful enough; and American designers were faced with the twofold problem of providing still greater steam-raising capacity while not exceeding the maximum axle loads that the civil engineers could permit. While much of American railway mileage was laid 'flat on the ground' as it were, the crossing of deep river valleys, and the difficulties in the mountain regions, had led in pioneer days to the construction of ingenious forms of trestle viaduct which, though cheap in first cost, often had a limited load-carrying capacity. It was in these circumstances that the Mallet articulated type of locomotive began to achieve great popularity, although like so many important inventions one feels that its original purpose was not along the lines that its major development ultimately took place.

In the latter part of the nineteenth century locomotive engineers in many parts of the world were seeking means of improving the thermal efficiency of steam locomotives. Theoretically the efficiency of the steam cycle depends upon the range of temperature and pressure through which the steam is expanded; and finding limitations in this respect when passing steam through one stage of expansion, as in an ordinary two-cylinder 'simple' locomotive, engineers turned towards two-stage or compound expansion. Many forms of compound locomotive were built, both in England and overseas; but the Mallet system involved the use of two separate engine units, under the same boiler. Two high-pressure cylinders drove one group of wheels, and the low pressure drove a duplicate set at the forward end. As well as exploiting the Mallet system of compounding, this layout enabled the locomotive to be articulated to a degree, keeping the rear engine unit with its axle bearings in the main frames, while mounting the forward (low-pressure) engine unit on a swivelling truck, which would provide some flexibility of wheel base, and enable the locomotive to negotiate sharp curves. Furthermore, by having separate engine units, each mostly having at least six axles, the total weight of the locomotive could be spread over many axles, and the individual axle-loading kept within the prescribed limits. One thus had in the Mallet articulated locomotive three attractive features: an articulated wheelbase; a spreading of the total load over many axles; and the possibility of using a very large boiler. I have mentioned the principle of compounding, because this was a basic feature of all early locomotives of the Mallet type. It was later discarded, and the enormous articulated American locomotives of the period 1925–40 described in Volume Two of this series, *Railways at the Zenith of Steam 1920–40*, had four cylinders all taking live steam from the boiler.

While main-line locomotives were getting ever larger, and some picturesque smaller units were being introduced for railways operating on substandard gauges in many parts of the world, the art of railway modelling was born. In its earliest days this development was almost entirely with steam locomotives, in many cases with wealthy patrons who could afford to have miniature locomotives running on lengthy tracks in large gardens. The cult spread to having still more extensive systems for conveyance of materials on large country estates. A locomotive enthusiast landowner would take immense pleasure from having the logging 'traffic' operated by an exquisite scale model of a Great Northern 'Atlantic' or a London and North Western 'Precursor', both of which in their full-sized form are illustrated in Volume One of this series, *Railways at the Turn of the Century 1895–1905*. The development of miniature steam locomotives reached its zenith in the years before the First World War in the passenger-carrying lines erected at various international exhibitions, and the famous model engineering firm of Bassett-Lowke Ltd. built some remarkably successful locomotives operating on the gauge of 1 ft. 3 in. How two of these found their way on to the derelict Ravenglass and Eskdale Railway is told later in this book. It was a venture that in modern parlance 'fairly started something'.

Reference to the building of private narrow-gauge railways in English country homes leads on to the subject of private saloons, and indeed of entire trains run in this era when railways were still the pre-eminent means of land transport. A number of particularly luxurious carriages are illustrated in this book, some for quite short runs like that from London to Brighton, and others for lengthy journeys in India and South America. One of the most interesting examples, typical of the period, is that of the use of the London, Brighton, and South Coast Railway's royal train to convey King Edward VII from London to Epsom for the 'Derby'. This train was originally built for Queen Victoria, when she made frequent journeys to the royal residence at Osborne, Isle of Wight. For the short run from Victoria to Epsom on Derby Day the engine was magnificently decorated (*see* ref. 77).

From the gaiety of such occasions as these, the period of this book leads on to that of the First World War, when the pre-eminence of railways took some unusual forms. Armoured trains had been used in the Boer War fifteen years earlier, but in 1914–15 they were provided for home defence in England. Then as the battle front became stabilised in France and Flanders a network of military railways was built up requiring large quantities of locomotives, rolling-stock, and even of track. Sections of line at home, used purely for peace-time traffic, were taken up and relaid 'somewhere in France' as the wartime saying used to go. At the same time some of the most important centres of the French locomotive industry fell into German hands. Many new locomotives were needed, and the immense resources of the British locomotive building industry, although diverting much of its capacity to the production of munitions of war, were able to undertake large contracts for the building of locomotives of French standard designs. In the later stages of the war American industry took a hand, and some interesting locomotives and rolling-stock took the road in France.

Large numbers of British railwaymen served in the armed forces not only in purely transportation jobs but in the fighting regiments. In the early days of the war there were no such things as 'reserved occupations' and many railwaymen who could later have served in their professional capacity enlisted in fighting units out of sheer patriotism. The 'Roll of Honour' of the British railways was a long one, and after the war the London and North Western, the premier line of Great Britain, and always topical in its engine naming, decided to create a 'war-memorial' engine. It was duly named *Patriot*, and specially numbered '1914'. Two further English railways followed this example: the Great Central with a large express locomotive named *Valour*, and the London, Brighton, and South Coast, with *Remembrance*. The idea was also taken up by the Great Indian Peninsula Railway, which named a new express locomotive *Hero*. These four make an interesting quartet, and they are all described in this book.

An important event on the continent of Europe just before the outbreak of war was the opening of the great new trunk line through the heart of the Bernese Oberland, involving the lengthy Loetschberg Tunnel beneath some of the highest ranges of the Alps. This was an electric line from the outset, but the beautifully styled façade to the tunnel entrance was typical of a period in which artistic elegance still played a major part in railway construction, and some famous English tunnel entrances are featured among the illustrations by way of comparison.

In previous books in this series some reference has been made to signalling in countries other than Great Britain. In this volume some typical French and American examples are included. The latter concern also the protection of level-crossings. At the present time equipment at level-crossings is also a live subject in Great Britain, when practice is moving away from the traditional fully-gated arrangement to the use of lifting barriers in the continental style. It is interesting to review in retrospect the methods commonly in use in the U.S.A. some sixty years ago. In one respect the situations in Great Britain and the U.S.A. were the reverse of the usual order of things. In Great Britain the use of fully-gated crossings was universal and compulsory where any public road crossed a railway on the level. The only exceptions were the private and occupation crossings in rural areas, where tracks connecting adjoining or other farm property crossed the line. In the U.S.A. the extent of warning and protective measures varied greatly from one railway and one state to another. These variations all helped to contribute to the fascination of world railways in this age of pre-eminence.

To maintain the continuity of theme it is not always possible to draw a strict date-line of demarcation, and one or two of the subjects relate to years just after 1919, while remaining essentially a product of the age with which the book predominantly deals.

1   **North Eastern Railway:** The 'R1' class 4–4–0.

2   **Chicago, Milwaukee and St. Paul:** Vauclain compound 'Atlantic' locomotive.

EXPRESS PASSENGER LOCOMOTIVE VARIETIES

AUSTRIA

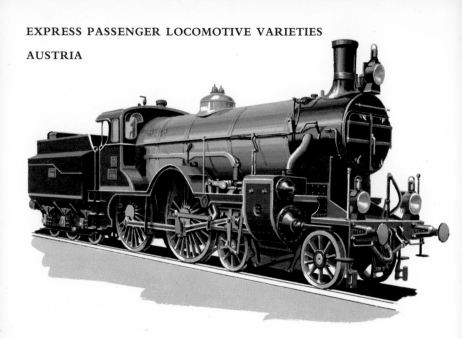

3 **Imperial Royal Austrian State Railways:** two-cylinder compound 4–4–0 locomotive.

ENGLAND (EXPERIMENTAL)

4 **Great Northern Railway:** the 'Vulcan' four-cylinder compound 'Atlantic' No. 1300.

5 **Prussian State Railways:** four-cylinder compound
'Atlantic' express locomotive.

6 **Baltimore and Ohio Railroad:** the class 'A3'
'Atlantic' locomotive of 1910.

HEAVY FREIGHT LOCOMOTIVES

BELGIUM

7 **Belgian State Railways:** 2–10–0 heavy freight locomotive.

INDIA

8 **North Western Railway of India:** heavy goods 2–8–0 locomotive.

9 **Atchison, Topeka and Santa Fé Railway:** 2–10–2
heavy freight locomotive.

10 **Great Central Railway:** the Robinson 2–8–0 heavy
mineral engine, later class 'O4'

GREAT WESTERN

11 **Great Western Railway:** four-wheeled high-capacity
wagon for bulk conveyance of grain.

GREAT CENTRAL

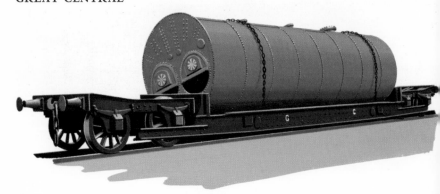

12 **Great Central Railway:** 25-ton well wagon.

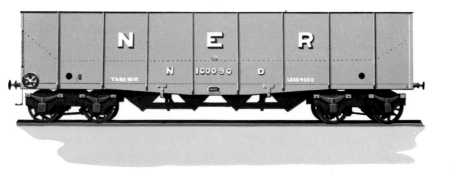

13   **North Eastern Railway:** 40-ton bogie coal wagon.

14   **North Eastern Railway:** high-capacity bogie covered
wagon.

15 **Ballycastle Railway (Ireland):** A 4–4–2 tank engine
of 1908.

WALES

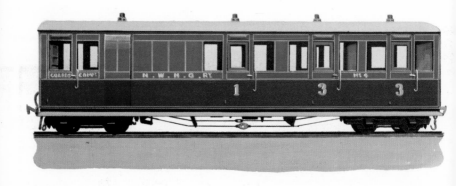

16 **North Wales Narrow Gauge Railway:** bogie-brake-
composite carriage.

17 **West Clare Railway:** 4–6–0 tank engine *Kilkee* of 1909.

18 **Ravenglass and Eskdale Railway:** 15-inch gauge 'Atlantic' locomotive *Sanspareil*.

HOLLAND

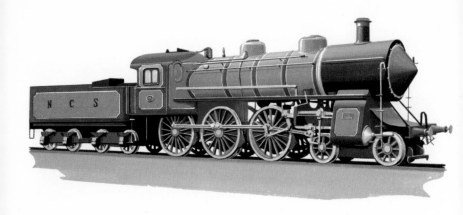

19 **Netherlands Central Railway:** four-cylinder 4–6–0
express locomotive.

HUNGARY

20 **Hungarian State Railways:** 2–4–4–0 Mallet compound freight locomotive.

21 **Prussian State Railways:** four-cylinder simple express passenger locomotive.

22 **Imperial Royal Austrian State Railways:** the Gölsdorf masterpiece, 2–6–4 express locomotive. .

MINOR RAILWAY AND SUBURBAN MOTIVE POWER

SOUTH WALES

23 **Rhymney Railway (South Wales):** steam rail motor coach.

NORTHERN ENGLAND

24 **Furness Railway:** 4–4–0 express passenger locomotive.

25 **Victorian Railways:** 4–6–2 suburban tank engine.

26 **Taff Vale Railway:** steam rail motor coach.

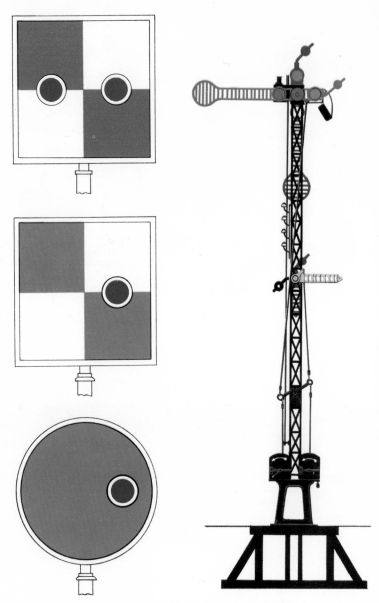

27–30 **French Railways:** some typical mechanical signals.

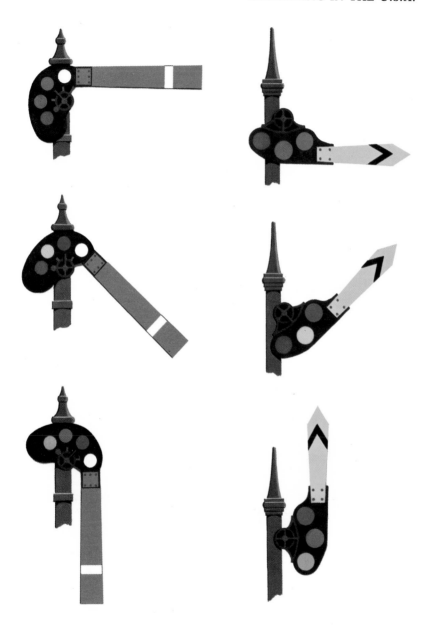

31 and 32 **Signalling in the U.S.A.**
Left: Lower quadrant semaphores.   *Right:* Upper quadrant semaphores.

33 **Somerset and Dorset Joint Railway:** 4-4-0 express passenger locomotive.

34 **Glasgow and South Western Railway:** a Drummond 4-4-0 express locomotive.

35 **South Eastern and Chatham Railway:** a Wainwright
   'D' class 4–4–0 express locomotive.

36 **London and South Western Railway:** the Drummond 'D15' class 4–4–0.

37 **Texas and Pacific Railway:** Class 'P1' 'Pacific' of 1919.

38 **Chicago, Milwaukee, St. Paul and Pacific Railroad:** the 'F3' 'Pacific' locomotive of 1910.

39 **Louisville and Nashville Railroad:** the 'K6' class 'Pacific' of 1912.

40 **Reading Lines:** high speed 'Pacific' of class G–2–SA.

41 **South Eastern and Chatham Railway:** Pullman car
for Continental boat express trains.

42 **South Eastern and Chatham Railway:** Pullman car
for Continental boat express trains (*interior*).

43 **Buenos Aires Pacific Railway:** family saloon coach.

44 **Buenos Aires Pacific Railway:** family saloon coach
(*interior*).

FURTHER CONTRASTS IN STYLE

ENGLAND

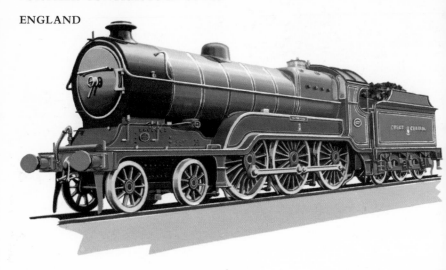

45 **Great Central Railway:** the *Sir Sam Fay* 4–6–0 locomotive.

SOUTH AFRICA

46 **South African Railways:** 'Pacific' type express passenger locomotive.

47 **Shanghai-Nanking Railway:** 'Atlantic' type express
passenger locomotive.

48 **Lancashire and Yorkshire Railway:** four-cylinder
4–6–0 express passenger engine.

EARLY DEVELOPMENTS IN ARTICULATED LOCOMOTIVES

AUSTRALIA

49 **Tasmanian Government Railways:** express passenger
4–4–2＋2–4–4 Garratt articulated locomotive.

U.S.A.

50 **Atchison, Topeka and Santa Fé Railway:** 2–6–6–2
Mallet articulated compound locomotive.

U.S.A.

51 **Denver, North Western and Pacific Railway:** Rotary snow plough.

ENGLAND

52 **Great Central Railway:** three-cylinder 0–8–4 tank engine for marshalling yard duty.

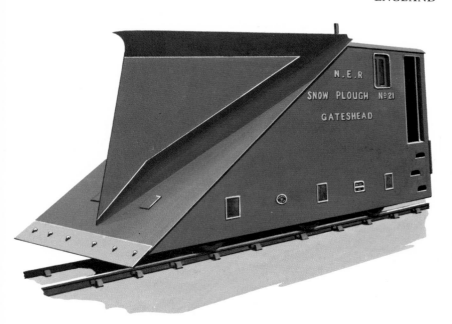

53 **North Eastern Railway:** locomotive propelled snow plough.

54 **Bernina Electric Railway (Switzerland):** rotary steam snow plough.

55   **Watford Tunnel, L.N.W.R.**: the south portal.

56   **Watford New Tunnel, L.N.W.R.**: the south portal.

57 **Shakespeare's Cliff Tunnel:** South Eastern and Chatham Railway, near Dover.

58 **Severn Tunnel, West End:** Great Western Railway.

COACHING STOCK VARIETIES

CHINA

59 **Shanghai-Nanking Railway:** third-class composite brake and mail van.

AUSTRALIA

60 **Victorian Railways:** first-class suburban car, with sliding doors.

61 **Bengal Nagpur and G.I.P.R. Joint Stock:** first and second-class composite carriage.

62 **Ottoman Railway:** first-class saloon carriage.

63　**London and North Western Railway:** the collecting
dog 'Buller', at Euston.

64 **North British Railway:** the Port Carlisle *Dandy*.

65 **Hump Shunting in Arabia**

FRENCH COMPOUND 'PACIFICS'

ORLEANS

66 **Paris-Orléans Railway:** the first 'Pacific' locomotive in Europe.

WESTERN

67 **French Western Railway:** four-cylinder compound 'Pacific' locomotive of 1908.

68 **Paris, Lyons and Mediterranean Railway:** four-cylinder compound 'Pacific' locomotive of 1909.

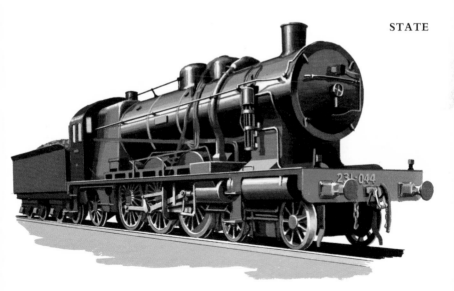

69 **French State Railways:** De Glehn four-cylinder compound 'Pacific' locomotive of 1910.

70 **London and North Western Railway:** Lineside postal nets.

SWITZERLAND

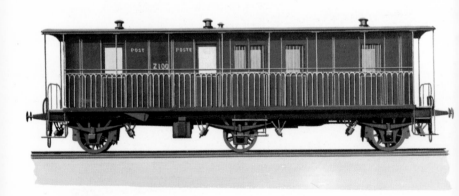

71 **Swiss Federal Railways:** six-wheeled mail van.

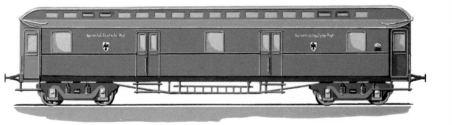

72 **Prussian State Railways:** bogie corridor mail van.

73 **London and North Western Railway:** Travelling
Post Office, mail exchanging apparatus.

DECORATED LOCOMOTIVES FOR ROYAL TRAINS

ENGLAND

74 **Great Western Railway:** engine decorated to haul funeral train of King Edward VII in 1910.

INDIA

75 **Great Indian Peninsular Railway:** 4–4–0 express passenger engine decorated for Royal Train workings.

76 **Midland Railway:** 4–4–0 express locomotive prepared
for the Royal Train.

77 **London Brighton and South Coast Railway:** 4–4–2
tank engine decorated for the Royal Train.

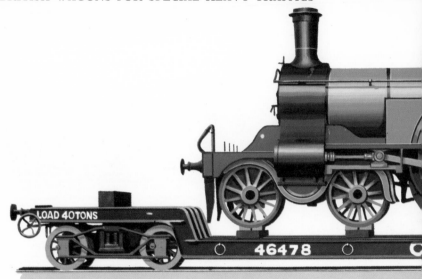

78 **Great Northern Railway:** 40-ton bogie well wagon, carrying locomotive.

79 **Great Northern Railway:** 20-ton eight-wheeled goods brake van

80 **Great Northern Railway:** 35-ton open bogie wagon
used for brick traffic.

VEHICLES FOR SPECIAL DUTIES

ENGLAND

81 **London Brighton and South Coast Railway:**
Inspection saloon.

INDIA

82 **The Maharajah of Rewar:** saloon car in his private
train.

83 **London and North Western Railway:** observation car on scenic North Wales routes.

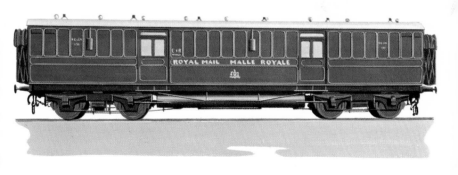

84 **South Eastern and Chatham Railway:** post office sorting van.

85 **Johore State Railway:** 'Pacific' type express passenger locomotive.

BRAZIL

86 **San Paulo Railway (Brazil):** 'Pacific' type express passenger locomotive.

87   **Egyptian State Railways:** superheated 'Atlantic' type
express locomotive.

88   **Northern Railway of France:** four-cylinder compound 'Pacific' locomotive (de Glehn system).

ENGLAND

89 **Lancashire and Yorkshire Railway:** 4–4–0 superheated express passenger locomotive.

ENGLAND

90 **North Eastern Railway:** 4–4–4 three-cylinder express
tank engine.

91 **North British Railway:** the REID 'Atlantic' express
passenger engine.

92 **Netherlands State Railways:** four-cylinder 4–6–0
express passenger locomotive.

SWEDEN

93 **Swedish State Railways:** superheated 'Atlantic' type express locomotive.

NORWAY

94 **Norwegian State Railways:** 2–8–0 freight engine, built in the U.S.A. 1919.

95 **Norwegian State Railways:** 2–6–2 suburban passenger tank engine.

96 **Danish State Railways:** three-cylinder 4–6–0 superheated express passenger locomotive.

THE 4-4-0 TYPE ABROAD

SWITZERLAND

97 **Swiss Federal Railways:** two-cylinder compound
4–4–0 express locomotive.

INDIA

98 **Madras Railway:** 4–4–0 express passenger and mail
engine.

99 **Great Northern Railway (Ireland):** superheated
4–4–0 express locomotive.

100 **Midland Railway (Northern Counties Committee):** 4–4–0 superheated express locomotive.

LARGER MAIN LINE LOCOMOTIVES

AUSTRALIA

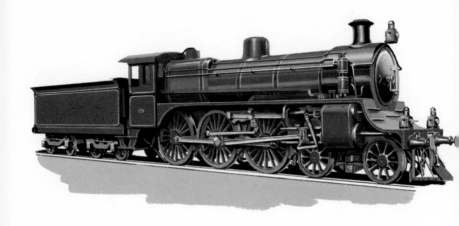

101 **Victorian Railways:** the 'A2' class 4–6–0 express passenger locomotive.

CHINA

102 **Chinese Government Railways:** 'Atlantic' express locomotive for the Taokow–Chingua line.

103　**New Zealand Government Railways:** the 'Ab' class
express passenger 'Pacific' locomotive.

AUSTRALIA (FREIGHT)

104　**Victorian Railways:** the 'C' class heavy freight 2–8–0.

105 **Lehigh and New England Railroad:** a 2–8–0 freight locomotive of 1911.

106 **Southern Pacific Railroad:** Cab-in-front Mallet compound 2–8–8–2.

107 **Pennsylvania Railroad:** the L1s, 2–8–2 heavy freight locomotives.

108 **Denver and Rio Grande Western Railroad:** a Class 'P–42' 'Pacific' of 1913.

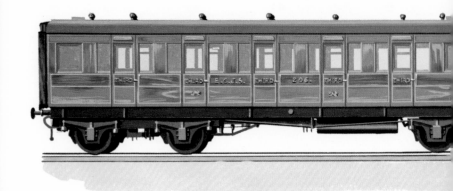

109 **Great Northern Railway:** Gresley articulated twin carriage.

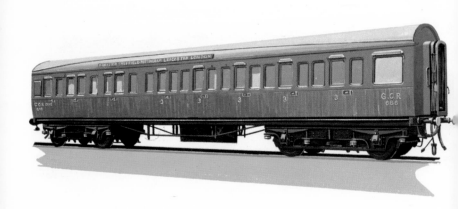

110 **Great Central Railway:** teak-bodied bogie corridor carriage.

111 **Midland Railway:** elliptical-roofed main-line corridor carriage.

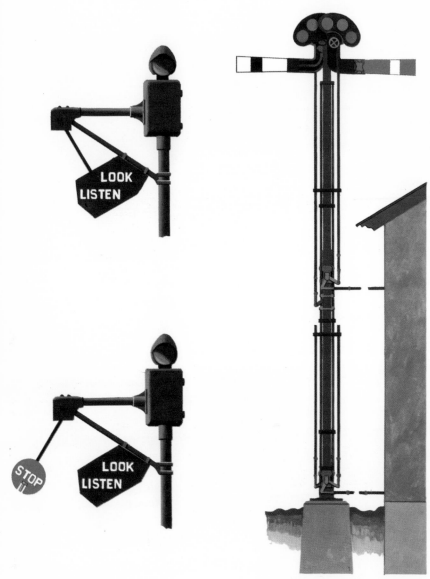

112 **Level Crossings in U.S.A.:**
the 'Union' automatic flagman.

113 **Manual Block Working in U.S.A.:**
double arm train order signal.

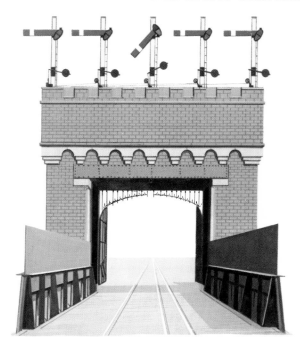

114 **Ouhd and Rohilkund Railway (India):** signalling at
Cawnpore Bridge over the River Ganges.

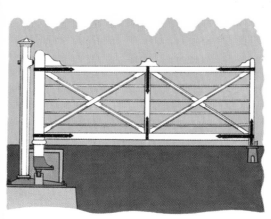

115 **Level Crossing Gate:** British practice.

116 **Level Crossing Wicket Gates:** British practice.

117 **Great Western Railway:** 2–6–0 fast mixed traffic locomotive.

118 **Caledonian Railway:** the McIntosh 2–6–0 express goods locomotive.

119 **London Brighton and South Coast Railway:** 2–6–0
fast goods locomotive.

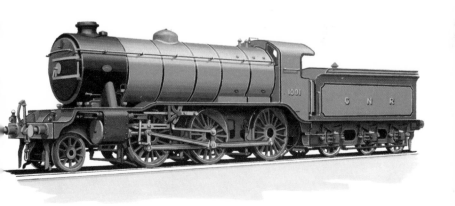

120 **Great Northern Railway:** the '1000' class three-
cylinder 2–6–0.

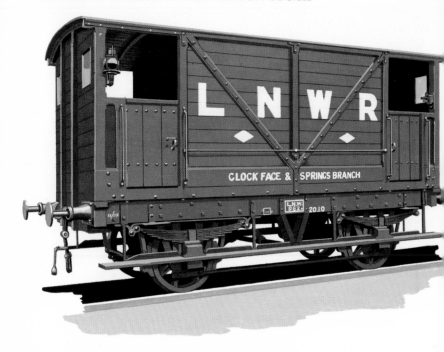

121 **London and North Western Railway:** Local mineral train brake van.

122 **Great Central Railway:** 30-ton all-steel bogie coal wagon.

123 **Great Western Railway:** 30-ton bogie covered van.

124 **London and North Western Railway:** cattle box for working on passenger trains.

125 **London and North Western Railway:** the 'George the Fifth' class 4–4–0 express passenger locomotive.

126 **Great Northern Railway:** the '56' class 4–4–0 express passenger locomotive.

127 **Midland Railway:** the '999' class 4–4–0 express passenger locomotive.

128 **Glasgow and South Western Railway:** four-cylinder 4–4–0 express locomotive *Lord Glenarthur*.

SOME STRIKING TUNNEL FAÇADES

SWITZERLAND

129 **Bern-Lötschberg-Simplon Railway:** the Lötschberg
tunnel, north façade.

ENGLAND

130 **Great Western Railway:** Box Tunnel, the eastern
portal.

131 **Chester and Holyhead Railway:** Bangor tunnel, western portal.

132 **London and North Western Railway:** Morley tunnel, the western portal, between Leeds and Dewsbury.

FURTHER LOCOMOTIVE VARIETY

SERVIA

133 **Servian State Railways:** 0–10–0 two-cylinder compound freight engine.

EGYPT

134 **Egyptian State Railways:** 4–6–0 express passenger locomotive.

135 **Great Southern and Western Railway:** 4–6–0 heavy goods and mixed traffic engines.

136 **San Paulo Railway (Brazil):** 2–8–0 freight locomotive.

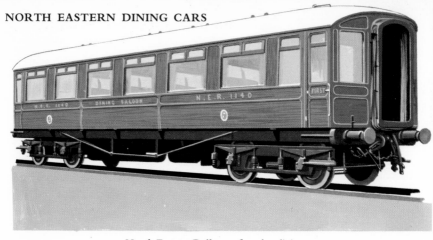

137 **North Eastern Railway:** first-class dining car.

138 **North Eastern Railway:** first-class dining car (*interior*).

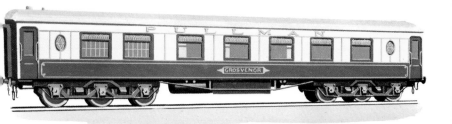

139 **London Brighton and South Coast Railway:** first-class Pullman car.

140 **London Brighton and South Coast Railway:** Parlour Saloon (*interior*).

BULGARIA

141 **Bulgarian State Railways:** 2–8–0 four-cylinder compound freight engine.

CHILE

142 **Chilean State Railways:** 4–6–0 express passenger locomotive of 1913.

143   **Gotthard Railway:** 2–8–0 four-cylinder compound freight locomotive.

144   **Bavarian State Railways:** Mallet compound articulated 0–8–8–0 tank engine.

145 **Central Railway of Brazil:** 0–6–6–0 Mallet articulated compound freight engine.

U.S.A.

146 **Erie Railroad:** triple articulated Mallet compound.

147 **Chicago, Burlington and Quincy Railroad:** a
2–6–6–2 Mallet compound of 1909.

SOUTH AFRICA

148 **Natal Government Railways:** 2–6–6–0 Mallet compound freight locomotives.

TANK LOCOMOTIVE DEVELOPMENTS

ENGLAND

149 **Midland Railway (LTS Section):** 4–6–4 express tank engine.

WALES

150 **Taff Vale Railway:** 0–6–2 general service tank engine.

151   **East Indian Railway:** 2–6–4 passenger tank engine.

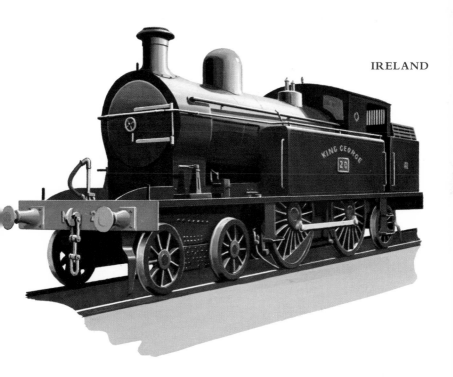

152   **Dublin and South Eastern Railway:** 4–4–2 fast
suburban tank engine.

TOWARDS STILL LARGER LOCOMOTIVES

FRANCE

153 **Northern Railways of France:** 4–6–4 four-cylinder compound express locomotive.

ARGENTINA

154 **Buenos Aires and Pacific Railway:** 'Pacific' type superheated express locomotive of 1910.

155 **South African Railways—Natal Section:** 4–8–2
heavy freight locomotive, 14th class.

156 **Italian State Railways:** four-cylinder 'Pacific' express
locomotive.

157 **Great Northern Railway:** 0–6–2 armoured train engine.

158 **Great Eastern Railway:** car for ambulance train, World War I.

159 **Great Eastern Railway:** 4–6–0 express passenger
locomotive in wartime livery.

160 **Railway Operating Division:** ex-Midland Railway
Kirtley-type 0–6–0 goods engine.

161 **French State Railways:** 2–8–0 heavy freight loco-motive.

FRANCE

162 **French State Railways:** four–cylinder compound 'Pacific' locomotive.

163 **The American Army in Europe:** 2–8–0 locomotive
for service in France 1918.

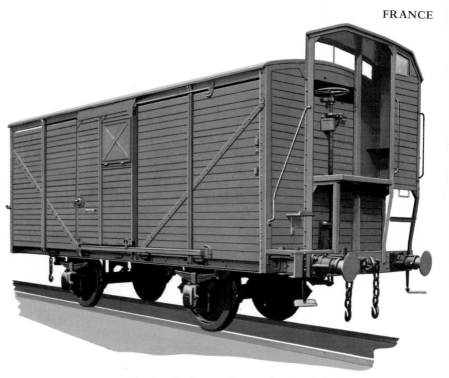

164 **Northern Railway of France:** American-built, four-
wheeled box cars.

165 **Madrid, Zaragoza and Alicante Railway:** American-built 4–6–2 express passenger locomotive.

166 **Northern Railway of Spain:** 2–8–0 mixed traffic locomotive of 1909.

167 **Madrid, Zaragoza and Alicante Railway:** 4–8–0
heavy mixed traffic locomotive.

168 **Northern Railway of Spain:** four-cylinder compound
'Pacific' locomotive.

U.S.A.

169 **Western Maryland Railway:** a class 'H8' 2–8–0 freight locomotive of 1914.

AUSTRALIA

170 **Commonwealth Railways, Australia:** 2–8–0 standard freight locomotive.

171 **Paris, Lyons and Mediterranean Railway:** four-
cylinder compound 2–8–2 built in U.S.A.

172 **Swiss Federal Railways:** 2–10–0 four-cylinder compound for the Gotthard section.

ENGLAND

173 **London and North Western Railway:** the War
Memorial 4–6–0 engine No. 1914 *Patriot*.

ENGLAND

174 **Great Central Railway:** the War Memorial engine
No. 1165 *Valour*.

175 **London Brighton and South Coast Railway:** 'dedication' locomotive No. 333 *Remembrance*.

176 **Great Indian Peninsular Railway:** War Memorial 4–6–0 express locomotive *Hero*.

LOCOMOTIVES OF THE 1916–1920 PERIOD

IRELAND

177 **Belfast and County Down Railway:** 4–6–4 express
tank engine.

ENGLAND

178 **London and South Western Railway:** the Urie
'N.15' class 4–6–0 express passenger engine of 1918.

179 **Highland Railway:** the 'Clan' class 4–6–0 express
passenger locomotive.

IRELAND

180 **Great Southern and Western Railway:** four-cylinder
4–6–0 express passenger locomotive.

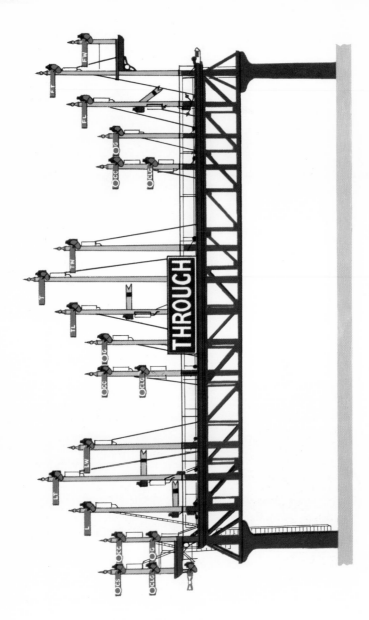

181 **Great Eastern Railway:** signal gantry at Stratford.

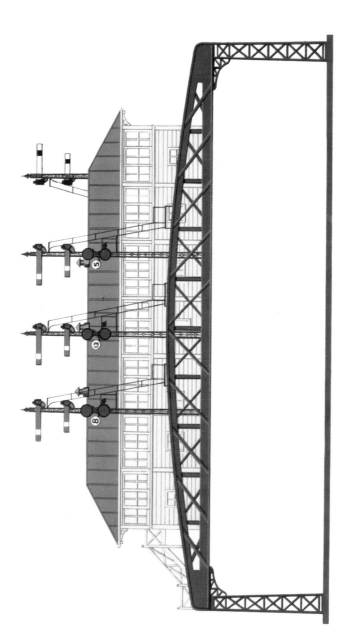

182 **Central Railways of Brazil:** Elevated signal box and signal bridge.

183 **Canadian Northern Railway:** 'Pacific' type express passenger locomotive.

U.S.A.

184 **New York Central System:** 'Pacific' type express passenger locomotive.

185 **Canadian Pacific Railway:** 4–6–2 type express passenger locomotive.

186 **Missouri Pacific Railroad:** medium-weight 4–8–2 mixed traffic locomotive.

INTO THE NEW ERA

AUSTRALIA

187 **South Australian Railways:** the mighty '700' class
2–8–2.

ENGLAND

188 **Great Northern Railway** (England): the Gresley
'Pacific' locomotive.

RAILWAYS

IN THE YEARS OF PRE-EMINENCE

1905–1919

1 North Eastern Railway: The 'Rl' Class 4–4–0.

At the turn of the century in Great Britain there had been a marked trend towards the introduction of much larger locomotives. Railway managements had made extensive overseas tours, and the memory of the Anglo-Scottish racing of 1895 coupled with the demand for much greater luxury in passenger accommodation had suggested that considerably heavier loads might have to be conveyed at the speeds of 1895. A variety of large 'Atlantic' and 4–6–0 designs was introduced in the years from 1900 to 1904, as noticed in the first volume of this series, *Railways at the Turn of the Century;* but the non-resumption of racing, and the development of improved design technique led to a strong revival in building locomotives of the favourite British 4–4–0 type. The North Eastern locomotive illustrated is a notable example. Ten of these very handsome engines were built at the newly-opened Darlington shops of the company in 1908–9, and for a time they monopolized the principal Anglo-Scottish services between York and Edinburgh, superseding the much larger 'Atlantics' built some five years earlier. In its original form the 'Rl' class was not superheated. It had cylinders 19 in. diameter by 26 in. stroke; 6 ft. 10 in. coupled wheels, and an unusually high boiler pressure, for a North Eastern engine, of 225 lb. per sq. in. Its work was as good as its splendid appearance.

2 Chicago, Milwaukee, and St Paul: Vauclain Compound 'Atlantic' Locomotive.

This striking locomotive was an exact contemporary of the English North Eastern 4–4–0 illustrated on the same page. Both were built in 1908, and they were alike in being the last of their type on their respective railways. On the North Eastern the 'Rl' was the last of a long line of 4–4–0s; on the Milwaukee the A2–c class was the last of the 'Atlantics'. The Milwaukee was an extensive user of compounds, and from 1892 there had been a succession of 4–6–0 designs, followed by some remarkably handsome 'Atlantics', in 1896 and 1901. The so-called balanced compound was introduced in 1907 with two high-pressure cylinders inside and two low-pressure outside. All four cylinders drove on to the leading pair of coupled wheels and this required a cranked axle. Inside cylinders and cranked axles have never been popular in the U.S.A., and in the following year the Milwaukee reverted to the Vauclain arrangement, as illustrated, with the high- and low-pressure cylinders arranged one above the other, and driving on to a single crosshead. Everything was outside. These fine engines were very successful. The cylinder diameters were 15 in. diameter high pressure and 25 in. low pressure, with a stroke of 28 in.; the coupled wheels were 7 ft. 1 in. diameter, and the boiler pressure 220 lb. per sq. in. The tractive effort was 22,200 lb.

With the extension of the railway right through to the Pacific Coast larger engines were required, and further developments were all with the 4–6–2 type (*see* ref. 38).

3 Imperial Royal Austrian State Railways: Two-cylinder Compound 4–4–0 Locomotive.

For more than twenty years the designing genius of Karl Gölsdorf was manifest in the motive power of the Austrian State Railways. Unlike many continental engineers of the day he endowed his locomotives also with a beauty of finish and dignity of line that was not characteristic of continental locomotives as a whole. The engine illustrated is a beautiful example of his work, dating from 1908. From 1893 he had built many highly functional looking two-cylinder compounds, which inherently had two different sized cylinders; but with the cylinders outside one could not see the queer effect of this, except when viewing directly from the front. The engine illustrated was also distinguished by a Schmidt superheater. All bright parts were burnished: the dome was of polished brass, and the boiler barrel was of planished blued steel. In appearance the engine is of particular interest as it marks the complete change from the earlier functional outsides to the grace and elegance that Gölsdorf adopted after a visit to England, and which reached its climax in his beautiful 2–6–4 engines illustrated in this book under reference 22. In the two-cylinder 4–4–0 the cylinder diameters were $20\frac{1}{2}$ in. high pressure and 30 in. low pressure, with a common stroke of $26\frac{3}{4}$ in. The coupled wheels were 7 ft. diameter, and the boiler pressure was 220 lb. per sq. in.

4 Great Northern Railway: The 'Vulcan' Four-cylinder Compound 'Atlantic' No. 1300.

This celebrated English railway had been a staunch upholder of the 'simple', or single expansion form of steam locomotive, and on succeeding Patrick Stirling as Locomotive Superintendent, and advancing from the 4–2–2 to the 4–4–2 type for his principal express passenger designs, H. A. Ivatt continued in the old traditions of Doncaster. At the same time compounds were being successfully introduced on several British railways, and the whole trend of design on the continent of Europe was towards compounds. Ivatt built a compound 'Atlantic' engine of his own, and at the same time the British locomotive building industry was invited to submit designs of its own for a compound 'Atlantic' engine to work on the principal Great Northern expresses from London to the North. The Vulcan Foundry was successful in securing the order for the trial engine, and the fine machine shown in our picture was the result. It bore a strong resemblance in its machinery to the De Glehn four-cylinder compounds in France, and did some good work on the line. Its operating expenses did not, however, prove superior to those of the ordinary two-cylinder simple 'Atlantics' of Doncaster design and build, and No. 1300, though a fine engine, remained the only one of its kind.

5 Prussian State Railways: Four-cylinder Compound 'Atlantic' Express Locomotive.

The various independent State Railways in Germany before the First World War were notable for the diversity and scientific nature of much of their locomotive practice. Running speeds were not high compared to the contemporary standards in Great Britain and France; but many features of equipment were being incorporated to improve thermal efficiency. The compound 'Atlantic' shown in our picture had a boiler barrel with a tapered section after the English Great Western style, and like the majority of German four-cylinder engines all four cylinders drove on to the leading coupled axle. This compound 'Atlantic' was not superheated, but the very wide and deep firebox will be noted. While this made for a lengthy and somewhat ungainly wheel spacing the ashpan could be cleared from the side of the track instead of from beneath, using a pit. The door can be seen almost at rail level. Although there were upwards of 100 engines of this type in use on the main line between Cologne, Hanover, and Berlin, the engine actually illustrated differed from the rest in being fitted experimentally with Lentz poppet valves on the high-pressure cylinders. All the rest had piston valves. The cylinder diameters were 13 in. high pressure and $22\frac{3}{4}$ in. low pressure, each with a stroke of $23\frac{5}{8}$ in.; the coupled wheels were 6 ft. 6 in., and the boiler pressure 170 lb. per sq. in. The total weight of engine and tender in working order was $139\frac{1}{2}$ tons, the tender being large to provide sufficient water for non-stop running over the 158 miles between Hanover and Berlin.

6 **Baltimore and Ohio Railroad:** The Class 'A3' 'Atlantic' Locomotive of 1910.

The Baltimore and Ohio was the pioneer railway in the U.S.A. and it attracted world-wide interest when the centenary of its incorporation was celebrated in 1927.

It was to these celebrations that the very famous English locomotive the *King George V* was sent. The B. & O. built up a fine record of service in its fast express trains between New York and Washington. For general working 4-6-0s had been used, in order to distribute the adhesion weight. This made it necessary to use narrow fireboxes. But the strengthening of a number of bridges enabled greater axle loads to be used, and so the newer express locomotives, from 1910 onwards, were built to the 'Atlantic' type, which permitted the use of the wide fireboxes generally desirable with the grades of coal most commonly used in America. The new engines, of which 26 were built, were two-cylinder simples and, as will be seen from our picture, fitted with a firebox extending almost to the full width of the cab. The cylinders were 22 in. diameter by 26 in. stroke; coupled wheels 6 ft. 8 in. diameter and boiler pressure 205 lb. per sq. in. The tractive effort was 27,400 lb. They proved excellent engines, but the rapid increase in trainloads led to their being superseded by 'Pacifics' after no more than three years on the principal express trains.

7 **Belgian State Railways:** 2-10-0 Heavy Freight Locomotive.

In the early years of the twentieth century there was much intense development in locomotives for heavy freight haulage. The development was far more rapid overseas than in Great Britain because on the 'home' railways the loading and speed of freight trains was limited by the absence of continuous automatic brakes on such trains. On the Belgian railways one had the combination of very heavy freight traffic and severe gradients in the mountain district of the Ardennes, and the very powerful 2–10–0 locomotive illustrated is symbolical of the demands currently being made upon motive power. These engines were built at the very old-established works at Haine-Saint-Pierre, the origin of which dates back to 1838. They were four-cylinder simples, with cylinders $19\frac{5}{8}$ in. diameter by 26 in. stroke; coupled wheels 4 ft. 9 in. diameter, and having a boiler pressure of which the exact English equivalent was 199 lb. per sq. in. The boiler was very large, with high degree superheating, and a grate area that was enormous for a European engine at that time, of $53\frac{3}{4}$ sq. ft. It was designed for burning the local Belgian coal, which is of considerably lower calorific value and quality to the high-grade bituminous coal then in general use in Great Britain. The engine alone weighed 98·4 tons in working order, and the tractive effort was no less than 45,635 lb.

8 North Western Railway of India: Heavy Goods 2–8–0 Locomotive.

The long association of the Vulcan Foundry of Newton-le-Willows, Lancashire, with the requirements of the Indian railways is typified by the fine example of a heavy freight engine shown in our picture. The period of the present book saw the setting-up of the Locomotive Standards Committee, which set certain principles for guidance in design with a view to standardization of practice, thus helping the manufacturers to obtain a better and possibly a cheaper product. The 2–8–0 illustrated was one of a series of which similar examples were introduced on a number of railways in the 1905–14 period. It had been usual for 2–8–0 locomotives to have the drive on to the

third pair of coupled wheels; but the Standards Committee recommended a drive on to the second pair. The North Western engine illustrated was one of the first to embody this recommendation. These engines had cylinders 21 in. diameter by 26 in. stroke, with Richardson-type balanced slide-valve, and inside Stephenson link motion. The coupled wheels were 4 ft. 8 in. diameter, and the boiler pressure 180 lb. per sq. in. Except for the louvred windows to their cabs, and the additional cab over the front of the tender, these engines were of typically British appearance. In later engines of the class the Walschaerts valve gear was used, and the drive was on to the third axle.

9 Atchison, Topeka, and Santa Fé Railway: 2–10–2 Heavy Freight Locomotive.

The 'Santa Fé', with a long and severely graded main line running from Chicago to Los Angeles, was an early user of ten-coupled locomotives for heavy freight service. Early examples of the 2–10–0 type introduced in 1902 lacked the flexibility of wheel-base needed for work on the sharp curves of the mountain divisions, and the design was modified in later additions to the stud to include a two-wheeled trailing truck. The 160 locomotives of this modified design, put to work between 1903 and 1906, constituted the first examples of the 2–10–2 type, which was appropriately given the class name of 'Santa Fé'. These engines were tandem compounds, and at the time of their introduction were the heaviest in the world. Our picture shows a later, and most important development; for the Santa Fé was one of the earliest American railways to break away from the prevailing fashion for compounds, of one type or another, and use instead a simple, massive and straightforward two-cylinder single expansion layout. These engines, enormous for the year 1912 when they were introduced, had two cylinders 28 in. diameter by 32 in. stroke; coupled wheels 4 ft. 9 in. diameter, and a boiler pressure of 170 lb. per sq. in. The tractive effort was 63,500 lb., and the engine alone weighed 132 tons. It is, however, significant of the rapidity with which locomotive size was increasing in the U.S.A. that within fourteen years the Santa Fé had engines of the 2-10-2 type weighing 180 tons without their tenders.

10 **Great Central Railway:** The Robinson 2-8-0 Heavy Mineral Engine, later Class '04'.

Although the Great Central Railway will be known to railway enthusiasts as a line that operated very fast express passenger services between London and the Midlands, it was primarily a freight-carrier with the core of its business centred upon the original industrial line which in 1899 constructed its extension to London—the Manchester, Sheffield, and Lincolnshire Railway. Under the skilful designing hand of J. G. Robinson the freight locomotive stud extended from the smart little 0-6-0 'Pom-poms' to large outside-cylindered 0-8-0s; and then to provide better distribution of the weight, and a smoother action when taking curves and turnouts, in 1911 Robinson introduced his famous 2-8-0s. For a massive freighter they were very handsome engines; but they also achieved a reputation of solid reliability that led to their being chosen as a War Office standard for service overseas in the First World War. No fewer than 521 additional engines were built and sent overseas to many different theatres of war.

The Great Central had, by the outbreak of war, 127 engines of this class at work. Not all those used for overseas returned to this country after the war, but numbers of them did temporary work on certain British railways, and no fewer than 273 were acquired from the Government by the L.N.E.R. after grouping. Our picture shows one of them in the original Great Central livery for freight engines.

11 **Great Western Railway:** Four-wheeled High-capacity Wagon for bulk conveyance of grain.

The vehicle illustrated is typical of the many wagons designed specially for individual traffic and built at the Swindon Works of the Great Western Railway. On that line the responsibility for locomotive, carriage, and wagon design and construction was vested in a single officer, and a notable degree of co-ordination thus achieved. In the design of special wagons for special traffics, as in the grain hopper wagon illustrated, its haulage by certain classes of locomotive was envisaged, and its handling at points of loading and discharge related to apparatus coming within the province of the 'Outdoor Machinery' section of the Chief Mechanical Engineer's department at Swindon. At the same time an interesting range of special names was devised for use in railway telegrams, and in parlance where traffic requirements were specified. Some of the code-names were appropriate, and easily appreciated by outsiders. GRANO, for example, could be readily associated with grain traffic. Similarly BLOATER suggested fish. Others, however, were purely code-names, such as DOGFISH for a permanent-way ballast-carrying wagon, a SIPHON for a bogie-covered van. On the other hand, INSIXFISH, could, with a little thought, be related to an insulated six-wheeled fish van!

12 Great Central Railway: 25-ton Well Wagon.

The years of railway pre-eminence were not only concerned with passenger services and the daily grooming of express locomotives as if they were about to convey royalty or function on any other special occasion. Large and bulky loads also had to be conveyed. The highways of Great Britain, let alone those of other countries, were not fit for heavy road haulage, even if there had been a means of traction available, and so the heaviest loads had to go by rail, when it was not convenient to take them by coastwise shipping. Sometimes individual consignments were too wide to be accommodated within the loading gauge, and then special arrangements had to be made for conveyance on Sundays, keeping both tracks of a double-line clear, and so loading the article that it overhung on one side. Many of the railways built a few special wagons to deal with such occasions, and our picture shows a typical well wagon, on the Great Central Railway, loaded with a large boiler for a stationary steam plant, such as might be used in electrical generating stations, or to drive the machinery in a large factory. The boiler shown would not encroach upon the loading gauge and so could be run in an ordinary week-day goods train.

13 North Eastern Railway: 40-ton Bogie Coal Wagon.

Export trade from the Northumberland coalfield was enormous in the years before the First World War. Heavy shipments went regularly to the Baltic States and to Russia, and rail transport consisted of short-haul shuttle workings between the pits and various small ports along the Northumberland coast that were specially equipped for the export of coal. Blyth was a case in point, and there, as usual in Northumberland, the coal trains were propelled up on to high wooden galleries, or staithes as they were known, from which the coal could be discharged direct into the ships berthed alongside. For dealing with the heavy traffic from Ashington Colliery about twenty miles distant, the North Eastern Railway purchased 100 special bogie wagons, each of 40-ton capacity, from the Leeds Forge Co. Ltd. These fine vehicles which measured 35 ft. $5\frac{1}{2}$ in. by 7 ft. $5\frac{1}{2}$ in. inside the body were designed so as to be entirely self-discharging. The end slopes were brought down at an angle of 36 degrees to the floor openings to facilitate the ready movement of the coal. The doors were arranged to move in a horizontal plane, and were opened and closed by means of a hand-winch and suitable gearing. These large wagons, which each weighed $56\frac{1}{2}$ tons when fully loaded, were not fitted with continuous automatic brakes, and were run in relative short trains. It was more convenient to have short trains and many of them shuttling to and from Ashington, than a few very long and heavy ones.

14 North Eastern Railway: High Capacity Bogie Covered Wagon.

The North Eastern Railway derived an overwhelming proportion of its traffic and great revenue from freight business, and the most careful attention was given to providing special rolling-stock for the most efficient transport of each commodity. The special bogie coal wagons for the

Ashington–Blyth export traffic provide an excellent example of this policy. For rapid conveyance of general merchandise a number of bogie-covered wagons were put into service. The limitations of the traditional British four-wheeled wagon were appreciated when it came to acceleration of service, and the large bogie wagons were not only designed to give safe and smooth running at speeds of 50 m.p.h. and over, but they were fitted with continuous automatic brakes so that they could be marshalled into passenger trains if necessary. The North Eastern Railway used the Westinghouse air-brake; but its working partners to the south and west used the automatic vacuum, and so these high-capacity bogie-covered wagons were fully 'dual-fitted'—in other words they were fully equipped with both forms of continuous automatic brake. They were 37 ft. long, and had a tare weight of 15 tons. They were designed to carry a maximum payload of 25 tons.

15 Ballycastle Railway (Ireland): 4-4-2 Tank Engine of 1908.

In the autumn of 1880 a narrow-gauge railway on the Irish narrow-gauge standard of 3 ft. was opened, covering sixteen miles of hilly country between the main line of the Belfast and Northern Counties Railway at Ballymoney and the attractive little seaside town of Ballycastle. It was not a very good business proposition, and the little independent company was in financial difficulties almost from the outset. Furthermore, these conditions led to 'making do' with inadequate locomotive power and rolling-stock. However, in 1908 a decision was taken to purchase two much larger engines, from Kitson's of Leeds, and one of these is the subject of our picture. They were large, and rather clumsy things for the little railway on which they had to work, and their 'modern' appearance rather belied their capabilities. They slipped so badly on the heavy gradients that their tractive power could scarcely be utilized. It was perhaps in keeping with a somewhat ill-starred project that payment for the two engines was long-drawn out, so long in fact that Kitson's eventually claimed interest on the money owing! After the incorporation of the various narrow-gauge lines in Ulster in the Northern Counties Committee section of the L.M.S.R., these Ballycastle engines were transferred to Larne and did many years service in goods and shunting work.

16 North Wales Narrow Gauge Railway: Bogie-brake-composite Carriage.

The outstanding financial success of the narrow-gauge Festiniog Railway during the nineteenth century led to a number of projects for other narrow-gauge lines, and some of these, it must be admitted, seem to have been projected with more enthusiasm than business acumen. The success of the Festiniog was derived from the existence of a large staple traffic in the conveyance of slates from the quarries of Blaenau Festiniog to Portmadoc for shipment. The tourist traffic, in which many visitors delighted in the beautiful mountain scenery of the district, was purely seasonal, and did not contribute a great deal to the revenue of the railway. The North Wales Narrow-Gauge Railway was constructed through the wild country to the west of Snowdonia where there was little in the way of staple traffic, and almost from its inception it was in financial difficulties. This did not deter the management from putting some remarkably fine passenger rolling-stock into service, of which the coach illustrated is a typical example. They were built by R. Y. Pickering & Co. of Wishaw, Lanarkshire, and were 30 ft. long over the bodies. The gauge of the railway was 2 ft. and the bogies were specially designed to give steady running

17 **West Clare Railway:** 4–6–0 Tank Engine *Kilkee* of 1909.

This fascinating narrow-gauge railway originated at the county town of Clare, Ennis, where it made connection with the Great Southern line from Limerick to Athenry. From Ennis it took a wild and meandering route to Lahinch on the Atlantic seaboard, and then southwards, always near to the coast, to twin termini at Kilkee and Kilrush. It was a line so beset by high winds that at times it was unsafe for the little narrow-gauge trains to run. There had been cases of carriages being literally blown over! From the turn of the century all new locomotives were of the 4–6–0 tank type. But the West Clare, like the majority of the Irish narrow-gauge lines was never very prosperous, and it purchased its locomotives one at a time: one in 1903, another in 1909, and a third in 1912. Far from being the same class they were all slightly different, and obtained from three different English manufacturers. The first was the *Lahinch*, from Kerr, Stuart & Co. of Stoke-on-Trent. The handsome little engine in our picture was built by Bagnall & Co. of Stafford. It had cylinders 15 in. diameter by 20 in. stroke; coupled wheels 3 ft. 6 in. diameter, and boiler pressure 150 lb. per sq. in. The total weight in working order was 36 tons. The similar engine supplied by the Hunslet Engine Co. of Leeds in 1912 was named *Kilrush*.

18 **Ravenglass and Eskdale Railway:** 15-inch Gauge 'Atlantic' Locomotive *Sanspareil*.

The Eskdale Railway, deep in the wilds of Cumberland, and only seven miles long, originated as a 3 ft. gauge line to convey iron ore from mines near the village of Boot to a connection with the Furness Railway at Ravenglass. Even at the best of times it was never very profitable, and early in the present century it ceased operation and the whole property became derelict from 1913 onwards. In the meantime a group of enthusiasts, whose activities were regularized by the formation of a company, Narrow Gauge Railways Ltd., had been enterprising the installation of 15-inch passenger-carrying railways at a number of pleasure resorts in various European countries as well as in Great Britain. The outbreak of war in 1914 put an end to the continental side of this business, but the N.G.R. took over the derelict Eskdale Railway, converted it to 15-inch gauge, and in the late summer of 1915 reopened the line for traffic. One of the locomotives was a beautiful model 'Atlantic' express type originally used at Oslo, Norway, and its arrival at Ravenglass naturally caused immense interest and enthusiasm. This engine, the size of which can be appreciated by the presence of the driver in our picture, weighed $2\frac{1}{4}$ tons, and was capable of running at 30 m.p.h. There were, however, very few stretches of this mountain line where such a speed could be safely reached.

19 **Netherlands Central Railway:** Four-cylinder 4–6–0 Express Locomotive.

This railway, which at the period of our book was an independent concern, formed an important link between the Western and Northern sections of the Dutch State Railway system. Its main line between Utrecht and Zwolle was only $54\frac{1}{4}$ miles long, but over that line some extremely heavy trains were run. The cross-country expresses, from west to north, included portions from both Amsterdam and Rotterdam. These were combined at Utrecht and handed over to the N.C.S. system. Then at Zwolle division again took place, and State Railway locomotives took separate portions to Groningen and Leeuwarden. The combined trains over the N.C.S. line were among the heaviest in Europe at the time, frequently loading to over 500 tons. The very striking 4-6-0s were introduced in 1910 for this traffic. They were built by the famous Bavarian firm of Maffei, in Munich, and as usual in Germany at the time all four cylinders drove on to the leading coupled axle. The cylinders were $15\frac{3}{4}$ in. diameter by $25\frac{1}{8}$ in. stroke; coupled wheels 6 ft. $2\frac{3}{4}$ in. diameter, and boiler pressure 174 lb. per sq. in. The booked speeds were not high: the 41·1 miles from Amersfoot to Zwolle were allowed 60 minutes start-to-stop. On such timings these powerful engines had a good deal in reserve, and records exist of time being kept with loads up to 700 tons (28 carriages). With their conical-fronted smokeboxes, and the wedge-shaped fronts to their cabs they became known as the 'Zeppelins'.

20 **Hungarian State Railways:** 2-4-4-0 Mallet Compound Freight Locomotive.

Within the vast extent of the old Austro-Hungarian Empire, as it existed until the end of the First World War, there existed a number of different railways, some run by the State, and others privately owned; and within those railways there was little standardization of locomotive practice. Reference has already been made to the work of Karl Gölsdorf on the Imperial Royal Austrian State Railways, and he exerted some influence on other lines, though it was an indirect and not a dominating influence. The engine illustrated shows one of the very few compounds of the Mallet type to operate in Europe—a design quite different from any thing in the Gölsdorf tradition. They were introduced for freight haulage in hilly country. The high-pressure cylinders, $15\frac{3}{8}$ in. diameter by $25\frac{1}{2}$ in. stroke, were at the rear, and the low-pressure, 25 in. diameter and also with a stroke of $25\frac{1}{2}$ in., drove the leading group of wheels. The Hungarian loading gauge permits of a very tall engine and the height of the boiler mountings rather take away the impression of a very powerful engine. The boiler was large and the firebox, with a grate area of $38\frac{1}{4}$ sq. ft., designed for burning low-grade coal. In working order the engine alone weighed 74 tons.

21 **Prussian State Railways:** Four-cylinder Simple Express Passenger Locomotive.

There are many points of striking similarity in basic design between this fine locomotive and the 'Zeppelins' of the Netherlands Central Railway (ref. 19). Both are four-cylinder simples, with the characteristic German drive on to the leading coupled axle, though the Prussian engine was built by the Berlin firm, formerly trading under the name of Schwartzkopff, but by 1911 known as the Berliner Maschinenbau Actien Gesellschaft. This German trend towards four-cylinder simple 4-6-0s with high-degree superheating was to have an interesting influence in Great Britain, on none other than the London and North Western Railway, when C. J. Bowen-Cooke adopted the same general layout for his famous 'Claughton' class engines of 1913 (*see* ref. 173). The great technical advantage is that the rotating parts are completely balanced, and there is no hammer-blow effect transmitted to the track. It is of interest to set alongside the comparative dimensions of the Dutch, German, and British variations of these four-cylinder 4-6-0s.

	Dutch	Prussian	English
Cylinders dia. in.	$15\frac{3}{4}$	$16\frac{7}{8}$	$15\frac{3}{4}$
stroke in.	$25\frac{1}{8}$	$24\frac{3}{4}$	26
Coupled wheel dia. ft.–in.	$6-2\frac{3}{4}$	6–6	6–9
Boiler pressure lb. per sq. in.	174	170·5	175
Total engine weight tons	71·2	76·5	77

The Prussian engine, by reason of its larger cylinder diameter, had the highest tractive effort by a small margin; though it must be added that neither of the continental types had to maintain anything like such fast schedules as those curently operated with heavy trains on the London and North Western Railway.

22 Imperial Royal Austrian State Railways: The Gölsdorf Masterpiece, 2-6-4 Express Locomotive.

One can say at once that these engines were among the most beautiful ever to take the road on the continent of Europe. They were also among the most efficient of their day. They were designed for fast express work on the main line between Vienna and Salzburg. Although this is heavily graded at each end there are, in the central areas, some long stretches where a good sustained speed can be maintained for scores of miles on end. This engine was also a compound, but on the later Gölsdorf system with four cylinders, all driving on the centre coupled axle. The high-pressure cylinders were inside, $15\frac{1}{4}$ in. diameter, and the low pressure outside, 26 in. diameter. The piston stroke of both was $28\frac{1}{4}$ in. The boiler was a very large one, with a total heating surface of 3147 sq. ft. and a grate area of no less than 48·65 sq. ft. These were enormous for any European passenger locomotive before the First World War. The coupled wheels were 7 ft. diameter, and to provide flexibility at the front end the leading wheels and leading pair of driving wheels were incorporated in a kind of leading bogie. To provide the necessary articulation in the side-rods the crank-pin of the leading pair of driving wheels was made in the form of a ball, which fitted into a socket in the coupling-rod. Many of these engines were built, and they achieved great success in service.

23 Rhymney Railway (South Wales): Steam Rail Motor Coach.

The need to provide economical transport on lines where passenger traffic was not heavy was a matter of much concern in the early years of the present century, when the costs of railway operation were rising appreciably. Where traffic did not warrant the running of more than a single coach on certain passenger services the practice of using discarded, or superannuated main-line engines was not economic, and the so-called steam-rail motor car became very popular for a time. Units consisting of a small, specially-designed locomotive and a passenger coach as a single entity were introduced on many railways. This particular example, taken from the practice of the Rhymney Railway, incorporates the important feature of having the engine portion detachable from the coach, so that the two portions could be serviced, or repaired in separate works, if need be. The passenger saloon seated 64 passengers. The unit was designed for working into remote districts of the Welsh valleys, and the car entrances at either end were provided with movable steps, which could be lowered almost to ground level when the unit was stopping at halts where there was no ordinary platform.

24 Furness Railway: 4-4-0 Express Passenger Locomotive.

The Furness Railway, making a winding course along the deeply indented coast of north Lancashire and then penetrating far northwards into Cumberland, is not, perhaps, generally associated with express running. But in the years prior to the First World War both the London and North Western and the Midland Railways operated a series of through-carriages to provide both for tourist traffic to the English Lake District, and for business travel to the shipbuilding centre of Barrow-in-Furness, and the numerous smaller towns where the famous haematite iron ore was mined. The trains conveying these through-carriages were smartly run, with a minimum of intermediate stops; and although the trains were not heavy by main-line standards, they required rapid acceleration from rest. Furthermore, in crossing the Barrow isthmus there were some heavy gradients. The new 4-4-0s introduced in 1914 were to the designs of W. F. Pettigrew, and were built by the North British Locomotive Company. They had cylinders 18 in. diameter by 26 in. stroke; coupled wheels 6 ft. 0 in. diameter, and a boiler pressure of 170 lb. per sq. in. They were not superheated. Painted in the distinctive 'iron-ore' red livery, they did excellent work on the line with the important tourist and business trains, often taking loads of 300 tons without assistance.

25 Victorian Railways: 4-6-2 Suburban Tank Engine.

The rapid growth in the suburban traffic of Melbourne in the early years of the present century led to the introduction of some very large and commodious new carriages, and a serious problem in haulage over the many steeply-graded suburban routes would have been created had not steps been taken concurrently to provide much larger and more powerful locomotives. The smart, very English-looking 2-4-2 tank engines were still doing a great job with the old rolling-stock; but six of the new bogie coaches, conveying in the peak hours 700 or 800 passengers per train, was another matter. The new 4-6-2 tank engines designed by Mr T. H. Woodroffe represented no half-hearted advance in engine power. They were, broadly speaking, a tank-engine version of the main-line mixed-traffic 4-6-0, and were in fact designed so as to be readily convertible to tender engines if the expected electrification of the Melbourne suburban area made them redundant before their economic life was ended. They had two cylinders, 18 in. diameter by 26 in. stroke; coupled wheels 5 ft. 0 in. diameter, and a boiler pressure of 185 lb. per sq. in. They were an immediate success, and put in many years of hard work on one of the busiest suburban services to be found anywhere in the world.

26 Taff Vale Railway: Steam Rail Motor Coach.

The Taff Vale, was at the same time the oldest, busiest, and most prosperous of the local railways in South Wales, but like its neighbour the Rhymney it had problems of light traffic at certain times of the day and at certain seasons. This railway was one of the earliest to introduce the steam-rail motor car. The locomotive engineer, T. Hurry Riches, was one of the foremost thinkers of the day on matters of railway traction, and was President of the Institution of Mechanical Engineers in 1907. His first essay in the way of railcars had been in 1903, and unlike the engine units on the railcars of other companies, the boiler was mounted athwartship, if one could use a nautical term. Riches was not entirely convinced of the desirability of using such cars for he found, as happened in recent years with some of the earliest diesel railcars, that the traffic department had a way of attaching extra vehicles to the railcar unit: a van, a truck, or even an extra passenger carriage. Then, of course, the diminutive locomotive on the railcar itself would be overloaded. Nevertheless, the steam-rail motor car provides a picturesque period-piece of railway development, and this later Taff Vale car is an interesting example of the 1907–8 era.

27–30 French Railways: Some Typical Mechanical Signals.

In referring to signalling on the French railways, it is important to appreciate that practice differed considerably on the five large privately-owned railways, and on the State Railway, as they existed in the period covered by this book. At the same period in Great Britain, while the details of the actual semaphores may have varied, it was only in the matter of subsidiary, and shunting signals that practice differed to any appreciable extent. At the outset, however, the difference between the most distinctive and familiar of all French signals, the red-and-white chessboard, carré (ref. 27), and the semaphore block signal (ref. 30) must be made clear. The carré is used entirely within the confines of an interlocking, as an absolute stop signal protecting points that lie ahead. If presented flat on to the driver, as shown in the illustration (ref. 27), it cannot on any account be passed. When cleared it is rotated about a central vertical axis and is presented edge-on to the driver. The most important variation in the use of the carré was on the State Railway, where it was used instead of the semaphore signal. The functioning of the latter must be explained before passing on to the other 'board' signals (refs. 28 and 29).

The semaphore (ref. 30) controlled the entrance to a block section. It permitted the departure from the area controlled by one signal-box to the next one down the line. At small country locations, where there might be nothing but a wayside station, or a single siding, the semaphores for both directions or working were frequently mounted on the same post, as in our picture. The semaphore arms normally hung vertically down, and were raised to the horizontal position and locked there when a train was in the section ahead and a second train could not be allowed to proceed. The semaphores were worked by handles at the foot of the post. The procedures for control varied on the different railways but except on the State

Railways, where the *carrés* were used instead, the indications as presented to the driver were generally similar. The small semaphore half-way down the post was of no concern to the drivers. It was for the information of signalmen only, and indicated the position of the semaphore at the next block ahead.

Some advance warning of a semaphore block signal in the danger position was of course needed, particularly for very fast trains, and the usual form of 'distant' signal—the equivalent of the English fishtailed arm—was a circular red disc displayed flat-on in the warning position. Some railways provided a second warning in the form of a green-and-white chessboard, as shown in the illustration (ref. 28). In the third illustration on the same page (ref. 29) is shown a green disc signal. This was used in certain cases to prescribe a speed restriction over a junction. It was, however, in these elaborations that the former privately-owned railways exhibited their principal variations. The Paris–Orléans Railway was perhaps the most individualistic of them all. That line, for example, never used the red disc as a warning for a semaphore block signal at danger; they used only the green-and-white chessboard.

31 Signalling in the U.S.A.: Lower Quadrant Semaphores.

In studying semaphore signalling practice on the American railways, one must first appreciate that the arms extend to the right, rather than to the left of the post, as seen by the driver. This is necessary because trains run on the right-hand track on a double-line section. We have chosen for illustration under this reference, and reference 32, examples of three-position

signalling, in which the one arm may indicate 'stop', ' caution', or 'proceed' to the driver. The successive diagrams show the three positions of the arm corresponding to these requirements of running, with the lamps shown red, yellow, or green lights at night. The arms illustrated, with square ends, are those used in station areas, and interlockings, where the 'stop' indication signified 'stop and stay' until the signal cleared. The 'stop and proceed' arrangement is explained under reference 32. During the period of this book there were a very large number of independent railway companies in the U.S.A., and while those that used three-position lower-quadrant signals conformed to the physical configurations we illustrate, the painting of the arms was not always the same. Some railways painted their arms yellow, with a black stripe, a forerunner of much later British practice for purely distant signals.

32 Signalling in the U.S.A.: Upper Quadrant Semaphores.

Towards the end of the period covered by this book, semaphore signals working in the upper quadrant were coming into extensive use in America. One of the great advantages over the lower quadrant was that no counter-weight was needed to return the arm to the danger position. From a comparison of the configurations displayed under references 31 and 32, there is little doubt which is the more distinctive indication, particularly in the 'proceed' position. Reference 32 shows arms with pointed ends. The 'proceed' and 'caution' indications have the same significance as those of an arm with square end; but in the 'stop' position the message to the driver is 'stop, and then proceed cautiously, being prepared to stop short of any vehicle or obstruction that might be sighted ahead'. From this meaning, the indication was known as 'stop and proceed'. This form of signal was introduced on a limited scale on British railways, from about 1925 onwards, but with colour light rather than semaphore indications. The degree of caution needed in 'proceeding' in such circumstances was not always fully understood by drivers, and there were instances of rear-end collisions. The procedure was never standardized in Great Britain.

33 Somerset and Dorset Joint Railway: 4–4–0 Express Passenger Locomotive.

Reference has frequently been made to the 4–4–0 type being the favourite British passenger design in the period just prior to the First World War. There were times when its use did not seem the most practical method of working the traffic, and at first sight a relatively small engine, with coupled wheels as large as 7 ft. diameter, might not have seemed an ideal engine for a line of such exceptionally steep gradients as those where the S.D.J.R. crossed the Mendips, between Evercreech Junction and Bath. Responsibility for motive power on the line rested with the Midland Railway, as one of the joint owners, and the engine illustrated is identical in every way with the standard Midland Class '2' superheater express engine, as can be seen by comparison of this picture with that under reference 77, which shows one of the Midland engines specially painted for working the Royal Train. Actually, despite their large coupled wheels, these 'Midland' 4–4–0s did extremely well on the 1 in 50 gradients of the Mendip route. They hauled six-coach

trains of heavy corridor stock, including dining-cars, without assistance, and even after they were superseded by larger engines for the regular workings they were much in demand for double-heading over the Mendips in cases of exceptional loading.

34 Glasgow and South Western Railway: A Drummond 4–4–0 Express Locomotive.

The Glasgow and South Western Railway operated in a compact area in the south-west of Scotland completely in accordance with its name, and as a business concern it was a tight little entity with very strong and closely-guarded traditions. In 1912, however, following the retirement of the much-loved and highly respected locomotive engineer James Manson, the directors appointed Peter Drummond to take his place. Drummond came to the G. & S.W.R. from the Highlands, but all his earlier associations had been with the Caledonian. That, to any 'Sou-West' man made all his actions questionable, for there was bitter rivalry between these two companies. In locomotive design Drummond reversed many established traditions of the Glasgow and South Western. He built much larger and heavier engines; he changed many detail features; and he changed the driver's position from the right-hand to the left-hand side of the cab. Once their prejudices were overcome, the men learned to appreciate the big, powerful Drummond engines, and the 4–4–0 class illustrated, and introduced in 1914, was exceptionally economical in service. They worked on the very hilly route between Glasgow, Ayr, and Stranraer, on which their comparatively small coupled wheels made them very suitable for strong and reliable hill-climbing.

35 **South Eastern and Chatham Railway:** A Wainwright 'D' Class 4–4–0 Express Locomotive.

Artistry in both line and finish of British locomotives probably reached its zenith in the various classes introduced by H. S. Wainwright in the years following the establishment of the working agreement in 1899, between the former South Eastern Railway and the London, Chatham, and Dover. The two companies were never amalgamated, but in traffic operation and all engineering matters their affairs were co-ordinated and regulated by a joint managing committee. It was, perhaps, appropriate that the express locomotives that hauled the continental boat expresses between Dover, Folkestone, and London should have been so splendidly arrayed, because for many travellers they provided a first introduction to the railways of Britain. They were not only handsome; they were strong and free-running, and in the period between 1905 and 1914 the boat trains, and particularly those carrying the continental mails were among the heaviest in England. It is a tribute to the design and workmanship put into these engines that many of them had a life of more than fifty years. They were not superheated. Their coupled wheels were 6 ft. 8 in. diameter and the cylinders 19 in. diameter by 26 in. stroke. One of these engines has been preserved and restored to its original beauty of finish and can be seen in the British Museum of Transport at Clapham.

36 **London and South Western Railway:** The Drummond 'D15' Class 4–4–0.

Dugald Drummond is one of the legendary figures of British railway history, and his younger brother, Peter, carried the family tradition on to the Highland, and Glasgow and South Western Railways. Particular interest is attached to the L.S.W.R. 'D15' class for it was Dugald Drummond's last locomotive design, before his untimely death in 1912. It is interesting to find that he, too, after building a series of large and imposing 4–6–0s, reverted to the 4–4–0 type for a high-speed passenger engine, albeit one that included a number of unusual and individual features behind its extremely handsome and neat exterior. For one thing he changed over to the Walschaerts radial valve gear, instead of the Stephenson, while instead of the popular form of superheating then being generally introduced in Great Britain, he used his own 'steam dryer'. This class, which consisted of ten locomotives, proved very fast and powerful, though Drummond's successor, R. W. Urie, greatly improved the performance, if not the appearance, but substituting a conventional form of superheater for the Drummond steam-dryer. These engines were used mainly on the Bournemouth expresses on which they did good work for more than twelve years. Their superseding then merely meant transfer elsewhere, and the majority put in more than forty years of good service.

37 **Texas and Pacific Railway:** Class 'P1' 'Pacific' of 1919.

In this, and the accompanying three illustrations, examples have been chosen of a variety of express passenger 'Pacific' locomotives operating on the railways of the U.S.A. The Texas and Pacific had an exciting start. It began as the Texas Western, and construction began as long ago as 1855. But it became very much involved in the Civil War; its tracks were torn up, its trains wrecked, and in 1871 a new start was made when a special Act of Congress was passed granting a Charter to construct the Texas and Pacific, and declared that it was a 'military and post railroad; and for the purpose of insuring carrying the mails, troops, munitions of war . . .'. It was never a prosperous concern, and in 1916 it went bankrupt. The rehabilitation programme that followed included the provision of fine new locomotive power, made possible by the extensive improvements made to the track. The new locomotives included 2–8–2s and 2–10–2s for freight, and the express passenger 'Pacifics' illustrated. These were very powerful engines for their day, having two cylinders 26 in. diameter by 28 in. stroke; 6 ft. 1 in. diameter coupled wheels, and a boiler pressure of 200 lb. per sq. in. The tractive effort was 44,200 lb. and the total weight of engine and tender in working order was 201 tons.

38 Chicago, Milwaukee, St Paul and Pacific Railroad: The 'F3' 'Pacific' Locomotive of 1910.

Under reference 2, mention was made of the extension of this great trunk line to the Pacific Coast. Until the year 1906 the western terminus had been at Evarts, South Dakota, a few miles east of the Missouri River; but in the previous year the westward extension had been authorized. This extension involved the construction of no less than 1400 miles of new line, through the heart of the Rockies, to Seattle. When completed the Milwaukee became only the second railway in the U.S.A. to run through from Chicago to the Pacific Coast on its own metals, the

other being the Santa Fé. For this vast extension of its activities many new locomotives were required, and for the fast through-trains three new classes of passenger engine were introduced all of the 'Pacific type. The first was the 'F3' illustrated. The 70 engines of this class had 6 ft. 7 in. coupled wheels, and were used on the fast stretches east of the mountains. The 'F4' followed, 20 strong, generally the same, but with 5 ft. 9 in. coupled wheels for the mountain sections. Both the 'F3' and 'F4', built in 1910–12 were originally non-superheated. The 'F5', of which there were 70, were the same as the 'F4', but superheated. All the 'F3' and 'F4' engines were eventually superheated. The 'F3s' had two cylinders 23 in. diameter by 28 in. stroke; boiler pressure of 200 lb. per sq. in., and a tractive effort of 31,870 lb. These 'Pacific' engines carried the whole burden of the passenger traffic for nearly twenty years, and it was not until 1929 that larger engines were introduced.

39 Louisville and Nashville Railroad: The 'K6' Class 'Pacific' of 1912.

The Louisville and Nashville was another of the very early railways of the U.S.A., and the present system has been built up out of a series of amalgamations. It extends in all directions of the compass from the parent stem represented by the two cities in its name, to St Louis, to Cincinnati, to Memphis, to Atlanta, and to the Gulf of Mexico with termini at New Orleans and Pensacola. During the Civil War the line between Louisville and Nashville was in the thick of the fighting, and it suffered accordingly. The present extent of the system dates from around 1915, and by that time there were some excellent engines on the road. It is interesting to recall that of the first 45 'Pacifics' introduced between 1905 and 1910, the majority were built in the railway company's own shops. Many more were subsequently added. The original design had the Stephenson link motion and slide-valves, but they were later rebuilt to have piston valves and outside Walschaerts valve gear. The engine illustrated is one of a batch built by Baldwins in 1912, for the former New Orleans, Mobile, and Chicago Railroad. This line was absorbed into the Louisville and Nashville, though the locomotives concerned continued to operate in their original territory. They had two cylinders 22 in. diameter by 28 in. stroke; coupled wheels 5 ft. 9 in. diameter; boiler pressure of 185 lb. per sq. in., and a tractive effort of 30,900 lb.

40 **Reading Lines:** High Speed 'Pacific' of Class G–2–SA.

The Reading System, or to give it the full title, 'Philadelphia and Reading', is a compact, very busy network in the States of Pennsylvania and New Jersey, an area where the density of population is twelve times greater than the average for the whole area of the U.S.A. Reading itself lies some fifty miles to the north-west of Philadelphia, but while the Reading System carried an enormous and diverse traffic, perhaps its best-known service, outside its own area at any rate, was that between Philadelphia and Atlantic City. It was over this run of 55 miles that the famous 'Atlantic City Flyers' were operated, and made a number of notable speed records. With the increase in train loads, due to heavier and more luxurious rolling-stock, it was necessary to introduce even more powerful locomotives, and the type of locomotive shown in our picture was

put into service just at the very end of the period covered by this book, in 1926. The crack 'Boardwalk Flyer' was scheduled to run the $55\frac{1}{2}$ miles from the Camden station in Philadelphia to Atlantic City in 57 minutes, and this involved covering sections of the route at over 80 m.p.h. These fine engines were two-cylinder simples, with cylinders 25 in. diameter by 28 in. stroke; coupled wheels 6 ft. 8 in. diameter, and having a boiler pressure of 230 lb. per sq. in. The tractive effort was 42,800 lb. and the total weight of engine and tender in working order was 218 tons.

41 **South Eastern and Chatham Railway:** Pullman Car for Continental Boat Express Trains.

The great success attending the introduction of Pullman cars for luxury travel on the London, Brighton, and South Coast Railway, since their first introduction in 1876, led to their use on the South Eastern and Chatham Railway from 1910 onwards. This line, like the Brighton, did not use corridor carriages for many of its main-line passenger trains, and no refreshment-cars were provided. It was considered that the relatively short journeys did not require this facility. In any case the situation could have been complicated by the inclusion of first-, second-, and third-class accommodation on all the principal trains. On the continental boat expresses there was certainly a need for accommodation of a more luxurious kind, with full buffet facilities, and the Pullman cars became extremely popular. Unlike the Brighton cars the external finish was made to match the standard carriage livery of the S.E. & C.R., instead of the usual chocolate and cream. The cars were named, generally to provide some association with continental travel, and the first six, introduced in 1910 were named *Corunna* (as shown in our picture), *Savona*, *Sorrento*, *Valencia*, *Florence*, and *Clementina*.

42 South Eastern and Chatham Railway: Pullman Car for Continental Boat Expresses (Interior).

The six original Pullman cars on this railway were of two varieties, three being of the drawing-room or parlour type, and three arranged as buffet lounges. Our picture shows one of the latter, giving the impression of a very pleasant club lounge. At about the same time a car of almost identical design was introduced on to the country services of the Metropolitan Railway, working between London (Liverpool Street underground) and Aylesbury. This became very popular enabling businessmen to have breakfast on their way to the City, and enjoy all the facilities of a club lounge on the evening journey home. The South Eastern and Chatham parlour cars were divided into three sections: a large saloon seating eight passengers, and two smaller saloons each seating four. These latter were much appreciated by private business parties. Additional cars put on to the Folkestone service were named *Emerald*, *Palermo*, *Regina*, and *Sapphire*. For the night service to the Continent via Flushing, a special car, the *Shamrock*, was put on for the provision of a full dining-car service on the outward journey, and of a typical English breakfast on the inward journey.

43 Buenos Aires Pacific Railway: Family Saloon Coach.

This very important line, now known as the Ferrocarril General San Martin, runs almost due west from Buenos Aires to Villa Mercedes where it made junction with the former Argentine Great Western Railway. From 1907 onwards the two railways were operated as a single entity under the management of the B.A.P.R. The two systems extended to the foot of the Andes mountains, with important stations at Mendoza and San Juan. It was built to the Argentine broad-gauge standard of 5 ft. 6 in. and, like all other major railways in the country except the Argentine State, was under British ownership. The total mileage of the B.A.P.R. and the Argentine Great Western together was about 2500. The lengthy journeys by the principal express trains involved the use of coaching stock affording the highest standards of amenity, and in addition to dining- and sleeping-cars up to the best British standards, a number of special vehicles were introduced that could be hired to parties, or used for other social functions that involved long-distance travelling. In 1910 there took place the centenary of the Argentine Republic, and at an exhibition staged in Buenos Aires the railways took the opportunity to put on display some of their latest and finest equipment. The B.A.P.R. exhibited, among other items, the family saloon car illustrated under this reference and 44.

44 Buenos Aires Pacific Railway: Family Saloon Coach (Interior).

This splendid carriage was built by the Birmingham Railway Carriage and Wagon Company, of Smethwick. Seating accommodation was provided for 21 passengers during the day, with berths for 10 passengers and an attendant on night journeys. At one end was an observatory, opening from a saloon provided with a fireplace with a white marble over-mantle. This remarkable feature, for a railway carriage, was at the opposite end of the saloon depicted in our illustration. The handsome easy chairs upholstered in green leather will be noted, and the apartment was kept cool in hot weather by an electric fan. There was no such thing as air-conditioning at that time. Beyond this very pleasant day compartment were three double-berth bedrooms, separate lavatories for ladies and gentlemen, and a bathroom, with hot and cold showers. The attendant's compartment was equipped with all the appliances needed for maintaining service in the main saloon and bedrooms, this equipment including an ice chest. Externally the carriage was finished in the standard style for main-line coaching stock on the B.A.P.R. If this carriage livery is pictured alongside the handsome green engine livery (ref. 15) it will be appreciated that the long-distance expresses on this Argentine railway bore a very striking resemblance, in colour at any rate, to those of the English Great Northern.

45 Great Central Railway: The *Sir Sam Fay* 4–6–0 Locomotive.

In the year 1912 the expansionist activities of the Great Central Railway reached new heights with the opening of the great new East Coast port of Immingham, by His Majesty King George V. For his enterprise, and the service to British exports to Germany and the Baltic that were expected to develop, the General Manager, Mr Sam Fay, was knighted. In the meantime, the general enterprise of the railway management had been matched by progressive developments in motive power, and when, in 1912, J. G. Robinson brought out a new series of very large 4–6–0 locomotives for

express passenger and fast freight service, the first of them was appropriately named *Sir Sam Fay*. They had the largest boilers yet seen on the Great Central, but at the same time a very neat and compact appearance. The two cylinders inside were $21\frac{1}{2}$ in. diameter by 26 in. stroke with steam distribution by the Stephenson link motion. This enabled all the 'works' to be concealed. Six of these very handsome engines were built, the remaining five being named after large cities served by the G.C.R., namely Chester, Lincoln, Liverpool, London, and Manchester. They worked on the through-expresses between London and Manchester, the crews lodging after each term of duty.

46 South African Railways: 'Pacific' Type Express Passenger Locomotive.

The diversity of working conditions for which locomotives of British design were applied could scarcely be better illustrated than in the group of locomotives shown under references 45 to 48: from the intensity of service in English conditions to the spacious open country traversed by the Shanghai–Nanking Railway to the immense distances, and sparsely populated lands in the Transvaal and the Orange Free State. It is remarkable, nevertheless, that the South African 'Pacifics' have proved by far the longest lived, and the present author has seen engines of this type in active service as recently as 1968. The 'Pacifics', built by the Vulcan Foundry in 1912, were put to work on the main long-distance runs from the cities of the Transvaal to the south and south-east, over the less heavily graded stretches of line. They worked, for example, on the Cape mails from Pretoria and Johannesburg to Kimberley. The two cylinders were 19 in. diameter by 28 in.

stroke; coupled wheels 5 ft. 1 in. diameter, and boiler pressure 200 lb. per sq. in. For the year 1912, they were very powerful engines for the 3 ft. 6 in. gauge, and the total weight of engine and tender in working order was 119½ tons—considerably more than the majority of British express locomotives of that period.

47 Shanghai–Nanking Railway:
'Atlantic' Type Express Passenger Locomotive.

This railway was a creation of the twentieth century, and in its construction and the design of its equipment British influence was very strong. Its main line from Shanghai ran for the most part through level country, and a finely-engineered and relatively straight track was built, on the 4 ft. 8½ in. gauge. From the outset the speed of the express passenger and mail trains was considerably higher than found in the majority of Asian countries at that time, and this was reflected in the large diameter of driving wheels employed. In the first volume of this series, *Railways at the Turn of the Century*, the remarkable single-wheeler type of engine, in Chinese Imperial yellow, was illustrated. Heavier trains required more powerful locomotives, and some 'Atlantics' of the handsome design shown in the present picture were built by the North British Locomotive Company. They also had large diameter wheels, 7 ft., and a very simple and straightforward general design. This railway had always favoured outside cylinders, but the steam distribution was by the Stephenson link motion arranged between the frames. The cylinders were 20 in. diameter by 26 in. stroke; and the boiler pressure 165 lb. per sq. in. The total weight of the engine alone was 66¾ tons, and of the tender fully loaded, 42½ tons.

48 Lancashire and Yorkshire Railway:
Four-cylinder 4–6–0 Express Passenger Engine.

The Lancashire and Yorkshire was in many ways a unique railway: it operated a swarm of very busy local lines centred around Liverpool and Manchester; it had an immense local goods traffic; and its interests extended to the great industrial cities of the West Riding of Yorkshire, and its maritime interests at Goole and Hull. Amid all this local activity it ran a large number of fast express trains, mostly of light formation, and the majority making many intermediate stops. A capacity for rapid acceleration was needed, with a good turn of speed between stops, and this very massive and impressive 4–6–0 design of 1908 was prepared to meet these conditions. It was a time when neatness of appearance was still something of a 'religion' among British locomotive designers, and to see one of these engines it was hard to appreciate that there were *four* cylinders, and that the valve gear for all four was neatly tucked inside. Perhaps there had been a little too much of the 'tucking in', because these fine-looking engines never really fulfilled expectations. They were not free-runners, and they were prone to mechanical troubles. Yet they represent an important phase in locomotive history that requires documentation. The cylinders were 16 in. diameter by 26 in. stroke; the coupled wheels 6 ft. 3 in. diameter, and the boiler pressure 180 lb. per sq. in.

49 Tasmanian Government Railways:
Express Passenger 4–4–2 and 2–4–4 Garratt Articulated Locomotive.

In this book frequent references and illustrations are made of the Mallet system of articulated locomotive. This was so designed to provide a very large engine unit, to be managed by a single crew, but to spread the dead-weight over many axles and thus avoid excessive loads on the track and under-line bridges, and at the same time to retain flexibility of wheelbase to facilitate operation on severely curved stretches of line. The Mallet, having driving-wheel units beneath the boiler, retains the limitation in dimensions inherent in the orthodox type of steam locomotive, while the immense length of some of these machines is itself a handicap. Except with oil firing, as in the case of the Southern Pacific 2-8-8-2s (ref. 106), one cannot put the cab in front. H. W. Garratt, a Government consulting engineer, patented, in 1908, the idea of having a single large boiler slung on a cradle carried on two entirely separate engine units, facing outwards. His patent was taken up by Beyer, Peacock & Co. Ltd. who realized the immense advantage of this arrangement over the Mallet. The boiler could be developed to ideal proportions, unfettered by any wheels beneath it. It could be kept short, and of large diameter, which is the best possible form for securing a high rate of evaporation. The firebox could likewise be as wide as possible. The very first Garratt articulated locomotive ever built was a small unit of the 0-4-4-0 wheel arrangement, for the narrow gauge sections of the Tasmanian Railways; it proved so successful that large passenger and freight locomotives were ordered from Beyer, Peacock & Co. Ltd. and it is the passenger engine that is the subject of our picture. It is, in effect, a double 'Atlantic' having 5 ft. 0 in. coupled wheels. A remarkable feature was the use of four cylinders on each engine unit, making eight cylinders in all. These were 12 in. diameter by 20 in.

stroke, and with all four cylinders of each engine unit driving on to the pair of coupled wheels adjacent to the cylinders a perfectly balanced engine was obtained as with the continental European 4-6-0s (refs. 19 and 21). This made for a very smooth riding locomotive. The total weight of the locomotive in working order was 94·5 tons.

50 **Atchison, Topeka, and Santa Fé Railway:** 2-6-6-2 Mallet Articulated Compound Locomotive.

The complications into which the designers of contemporary Mallet articulated locomotives could become involved could not be better illustrated than by the Santa Fé 2-6-6-2 shown in our picture. This was one of a batch of 40, built by the Baldwin Locomotive Company, and designed to work trains of about 2500 tons up a gradient of 1 in 166 at 15 m.p.h. The immensely long boiler was built in two sections connected by a combustion chamber 5 ft. long. The ordinary flue tubes were in the rear section, while in the front section were a reheater, superheater, and feed water-heater. In 38 engines of the class the two sections of the boiler were rigidly connected, making an assembly nearly 38 ft. long! The remaining two engines had flexible connections between the two parts of the boiler, thereby allowing the front part to be rigidly attached to the leading frame in the articulation, while the rear part was attached to the rear frame in the usual way. One locomotive was fitted with a bellows joint between the two sections of the boiler, and the locomotive shown in our picture was fitted with a double ball joint. The fact that these complicated devices were not perpetuated in any future design probably tells its own tale. Otherwise all 40 engines of the class were similar in having cylinder diameters of 24 in. high pressure, 38 in. low pressure, the stroke in each being 28 in.; the coupled wheel diameter was unusually large for an engine designed for slow-speed service, namely 5 ft. 9 in. The boiler pressure was 200 lb. per sq. in., and the total weight of engine and tender in working order was 251 tons.

51 Denver, North Western, and Pacific Railway: Rotary Snow Plough.

Keeping the line of a railway clear in times of heavy snowfall is a difficult enough operation even in the temperate climate of the British Isles; but in countries of very severe winters, in Switzerland, Scandinavia, and above all in North America the ordinary pusher-plough (ref. 53) would be useless. For work in the most severe conditions the rotary form of snow plough was introduced on the Union Pacific Railroad in the U.S.A. and our picture illustrates a later version put into service in 1906–7. The railroad in question is now part of the Denver and Rio Grande Western. In service a deep snow-drift was simply cut through by the revolving scoops and thrown away to one side. There was no question of 'charging' a drift. The plough was propelled by two or more locomotives, and the power to actuate the rotary cutters was derived from a pair of horizontal cylinders receiving steam from an ordinary loco-motive-type boiler mounted in the 'house' behind the rotary cutters. One of these ploughs in action presented a most spectacular sight. Sometimes the general level of the snow would be almost up to

the carriage roofs, and the plough and its own 'engine' belching exhaust steam, and three engines propelling, would be practically invisible, behind the whirlwind of snow being cut from the line of railway and hurled well clear to one side.

52 Great Central Railway: Three-cylinder 0–8–4 Tank Engine for Marshalling Yard Duty.

These huge engines, three of which were built by Beyer, Peacock & Co. Ltd. in 1908, and which weighed $96\frac{1}{2}$ tons, were a further example of the Great Central tradition for 'thinking big'. A huge new marshalling yard had been laid down at Wath, near Barnsley, for classification of traffic from the south Yorkshire coalfield. It was designed on the 'hump' principle and powerful locomotives were needed for propelling the heavy trains up the steep gradient leading to the hump. The use of three cylinders in these locomotives postulated an important principle. There were six exhausts from the chimney for each revolution of the driving wheels, and these made for a more 'even' torque in the application of the cylinder power to the turning of the driving wheels, and less liability to slipping. The three cylinders were 18 in. diameter by 26 in. stroke, with the inside cylinder driving the second axle, and the two outside cylinders the third. These engines, although engaged wholly on shunting, were provided with large coal and water capacity, so that they could continue at work for days on end without the need for constant replenishment. It is a tribute to the success of these engines of 1908 that two further examples were built new by the L.N.E.R. in 1932, with the important addition of booster units.

53 North Eastern Railway: Loco-motive Propelled Snow Plough.

The clearing of snow from a railway track can at times be a hazardous business. Conditions in Great Britain rarely reach the degree of severity as to need rotary types of snow plough as illustrated under references 51 and 54 in this book, and the type of plough shown in the present picture has usually proved adequate. There is, nevertheless, a point in choosing the North Eastern plough for illustration. Wilson Worsdell, the Locomotive Super-intendent, had specified a 'good solid house' because the propelling force of two or three locomotives when bucking into a snow-drift could be considerable. Yet on one occasion the 'good solid house' was not enough. One winter's night in 1888 the 'Flying Scotsman' had become stuck in a snow-drift near Longhirst, about twenty miles north of Newcastle. A relief expedi-tion, consisting of snow plough propelled by four engines, set out; but in the breakdown of communications caused by the blizzard, and a misjudgement of distance, the snow plough propelled by its four engines collided with another train facing in the opposite direction, which had also become completely stuck in another snow-drift. The snow plough 'house', caught between its own four engines, and the two engines of the standing train was almost completely destroyed. Of the five men inside, three were no more than slightly injured, but one died of his injuries. Wilson Worsdell himself, though seriously injured, re-covered later.

54 Bernina Electric Railway (Swit-zerland): Rotary Steam Snow Plough. The Bernina Electric Railway climbing from St Moritz to the Bernina Hospice station 7400 ft. above sea-level, attains the highest altitude of any railway in Europe other than rack systems. As might be expected, snow conditions in winter are exceptionally severe, and when the railway was first opened small snow ploughs operated by the electric passenger motor coaches were tried. These proved ineffec-tive in the worst conditions. The gradients in places are as steep as 1 in 14, and the power needed to clear snow and climb the gradient required an output of about 1000 horse-power. It was not possible to draw such a power from the overhead line, and a remarkable rotary steam snow plough was built for this metre-gauge railway by the Swiss Locomotive Works at Winterthur. The large steam boiler pro-vides steam for three separate engine units. Two are a kind of hybrid Mallet, but with the four cylinders close together in the middle, and the third drives the rotary plough. This latter has cylinders $11\frac{13}{16}$ in. diameter by $17\frac{3}{4}$ in. stroke, and through gearing causes the rotary cutter to revolve at 170 revolutions per minute. The propelling engines have cylinders of the same diameter but only $13\frac{3}{4}$ in. stroke. The coupled-wheel diameter is 2 ft. $5\frac{1}{2}$ in. The working pressure in the large boiler is 176 lb. per sq. in. Behind the locomotive is a four-wheeled tender. When working the whole outfit is enclosed in a rectangular casing large enough to allow a man to pass along either side of the boiler. The Bernina Railway was opened in 1910, and since that time the snow-clearing apparatus has proved very effective. For many years there was a snow-gauge at the Bernina Hospice station showing the depths of snow through which they had successfully worked the trains. Cross-bars were fixed on the post for various winters of exceptional severity, and the maximum crossbar mark showed that in this particular winter trains had been worked through 20 ft. 9 in. of snow! The plough shown in our picture had cut channels of this depth through solid ice and snow, through which the little electric trains had passed in vertical-sided cuttings of glistening white.

55 Watford Tunnel, L.N.W.R.: The South Portal.

On the early railways, designed on easy gradients so as not to present difficult haulage problems to the primitive locomotives of the day, it was necessary to construct many long tunnels where the lines ran athwart ranges of hills, and the London and Birmingham Railway built by Robert Stephenson provides a typical example. The earliest trains included a number of open carriages, from which passengers could appreciate to the full the engineering and architectural features of the line. It is to be feared that those in the open carriages would be more in the mood for protecting themselves from the weather, and from smoke and cinders thrown out by the locomotive. For whatever reasons, however, it became the fashion to adorn tunnel entrances with quite elaborate façades, some of which were of definite architectural merit. The entrance to Watford Tunnel has a splendid classical portico, but for some reason—possibly economy in construction—the wing walls extending to the slopes of the cutting are in red brick. The façade remains unchanged today, though much weathered, and blackened with a hundred years of steam traction, while the cutting sides are much covered with trees and the wing walls can scarcely be seen.

56 Watford New Tunnel L.N.W.R.: The South Portal.

The original London and Birmingham main line, under London and North Western management, grew to be the busiest in all England, and even before the end of the nineteenth century the original double-tracked line was proving inadequate. In 1874 the 'new' line was opened, with a new double-line tunnel running parallel to the old one through the hills north of Watford. The interesting difference between style of the façade will be noted, and also the shape of the actual tunnel arch. It may be added that the 'new' tunnel had to be located some little distance to the east of the original tunnel, so as to avoid any geological disturbance. In consequence the new tunnel had to be approached in a series of reverse curves. This was of no matter since the new tunnel was used by the goods trains and the local passenger services. The fast expresses used the original tunnel, which both in its approaches and throughout its length is straight. The modern electric trains pass through the original tunnel at speeds up to 100 m.p.h.

57 Shakespeare's Cliff Tunnel: South Eastern and Chatham Railway, near Dover.

The main line to Dover, engineered by William Cubitt, was one of the great pioneer lines of England. Between Folkestone and Dover it is carried through the range of chalk cliffs—the White Cliffs of Dover—that are famed in song and story. Picturesque they may be, but they set a rare problem to the engineers when it came to building a railway through them! Nowhere did the terrain give rise to more concern than in the last miles before Dover, where the line had to be tunnelled under

Shakespeare's cliff, on the edge of which was enacted the great scene in *King Lear*. So concerned was Cubitt about the stability of the chalk at this point that he abandoned the usual form of arch for tunnel construction, and adopted the two parallel tunnels with tall pointed bores, like Gothic arches. As such it became one of the most distinctive tunnels anywhere in the world. Whatever apprehension Cubitt may have had his work, completed in 1843, stands four-square today. It has witnessed more than a hundred years of steam traction, and today carries electric trains, and the occasional diesel. It is straight throughout, and in our picture the further end can be discerned in the left-hand bore.

58 Severn Tunnel, West End: Great Western Railway.

The Severn Tunnel, built to shorten the route from London and Bristol to South Wales by some twenty miles, is a 'period piece' in railways; not so much in its design nor in the extraordinary series of difficulties that were encountered in its construction, but in the fundamental decision to build a tunnel at all beneath the estuary of the River Severn. One doubts if a tunnel would have been chosen, had the railway been built in the present age. It was opened in 1886, but it was not until the construction of the South Wales direct line, via Badminton, that its full importance was exploited. Then the traffic that developed, in the period of the present book, became something of an embarrassment. The heavy coal trains from South Wales all required two engines to surmount the severe gradients leading out of the tunnel. Ventilation has always been a problem, and a huge pumping station has to be maintained on the Monmouthshire side to keep the tunnel clear of water. It is the longest tunnel in Great Britain, four miles long; and interesting as are all the problems connected with its operation and maintenance one feels, wise after the event, that a bridge would have been preferable to a tunnel!

59 Shanghai–Nanking Railway: Third-Class Composite Brake and Mail Van.

Under reference 47 the physical characteristics of this twentieth-century railway were mentioned, to the extent that they affected the locomotive stock. The present picture illustrates a coach from one of the beautiful trains introduced when the line was first opened. Like the locomotive stock, all the original orders for carriages and wagons were executed in Great Britain. Five vestibuled corridor trains were built by the then Metropolitan Amalgamated Carriage and Wagon Company, at Saltley, Birmingham. Each train consisted of six coaches, each of five different types in the one train: third brake, luggage and mail (as illustrated); vestibuled third; first- and second-class composite; first, kitchen car; and third brake van. The splendid external finish, with the panels in Chinese Imperial yellow, will be apparent from our picture; the interior of the cars was finished in polished pitch pine. They were lengthy vehicles, 68 ft. over the headstocks, and the generous loading gauge of this new railway permitted them to be built tall. The third-class cars seated 100 in the vestibuled saloon, 60 in the brake composite, and 40 in the composite brake luggage and mail car illustrated. The trains were electrically lighted throughout. It can be well imagined what a handsome sight one of these six-car trains would present, hauled by an immaculate green engine like that shown under reference 47.

60 Victorian Railways: First-Class Suburban Car, With Sliding Doors.

Under reference 25, the circumstances that led to a complete modernization of loco-motive power and rolling-stock in the Melbourne suburban area were described. Having considered the effects of this on motive power one of the new coaches is illustrated herewith. They were of what was then a novel design, for while follow-ing the cross-compartment principle, sliding doors were used. Means of com-munication were provided by a central gangway instead of by a side corridor. It is amusing to recall that these doors were not generally welcomed on their first intro-duction. Passengers did not trouble to close them in warm weather, and then, as the train was approaching a station, and passengers were preparing to alight, the rapid decelerative effect caused open doors to shut, just as they were required to be open! This was overcome by the fitting of self-acting latches whereby the doors were held either open or closed, and did not slide about willy-nilly. The need to have ample space for entering and leaving was paramount. The London Underground railways could not teach Melbourne any-thing in the way of rapid stops at stations. On the majority of routes the station stops were about 15 seconds, and with the powerful 4–6–2 tank engines subsequent acceleration was rapid.

61 Bengal Nagpur and G.I.P.R. Joint Stock: First and Second-class Composite Carriage.

Reference is made elsewhere in this book to coaching stock operated on joint express

train services, and the fine vehicle illus-trated is a good example of such practice in India. The mail and express passenger traffic between the great cities of Bombay and Calcutta was jointly worked by the Great Indian Peninsula and the Bengal Nagpur Railways, and some interesting vehicles were built specially for the purpose. The steel underframes and bogies were built in England by the Metropolitan Amalgamated Carriage and Wagon Com-pany of Saltley, while of the bodies some were built by the G.I.P. Railway and some by the Bengal Nagpur. All the painting was done by the latter, in the standard livery of that company. The coaches were of various types, providing first-, second-, and third-class accommodation, and were fitted throughout with electric light and electric ventilating fans. The stock was unusual in Indian practice of the day in having corridors and vestibules for the third-class portions of the trains. As originally built, and as illustrated in our picture, the carriages had continuous foot-boards and continuous handrails; but those were times of certain unrest in India, and to minimize the risk of assault and train robbery the footboards and handrails were subsequently removed.

62 Ottoman Railway: First-class Saloon Carriage.

This railway, operating from Smyrna, in the old Turkish Empire, purchased much of its rolling-stock from Great Britain. The locomotives, apart from their head-lights and large cabs, could easily have belonged to an English railway from their appearance at any rate; but the British-built coaching stock naturally included a number of features suitable for use in an

Oriental country. The handsome saloon carriages, built by the Gloucester Railway Carriage and Wagon Co., were of the open type with seating for sixty first-class passengers. The seats were of the 'walkover' type, so that passengers could sit facing or back to the engine as they pleased, and they were covered with rattan. It is evident that these cars were not intended for long-distance service, as the space for luggage was confined to small basket racks. At a time when many British railways were still wholly dependent upon gas lighting for passenger carriages these Turkish cars were electrically lit, and had the open platforms at the ends also lighted. Structurally, the body framing was of teak, but the roof framing was of English oak. The bodies were built separately from the steel under-frames. The length of the cars, over the corner pillars, was 43 ft. 6 in.

63 London and North Western Railway: The Collecting Dog, 'Buller', at Euston.

In these utilitarian days it seems hard to imagine a time when the departure of an express train from a leading London terminus would be preceded, ten minutes or so before the start, by a large and friendly dog nosing its way into each compartment, and by the sheer force of its lovable character securing many contributions for the collecting-box on its back. For many years 'Buller' was as familiar a feature of the bustling animated scene at Euston as the Doric Arch, or the magnificent architecture of the Great Hall—perhaps even more so, because the majority of main-line travellers could not escape the attentions of 'Buller', whereas the architectural features of the station went unheeded. 'Buller' collected on behalf of the London and North Western Railway Servants' Benevolent Fund. He took up his job on the platforms at Euston in 1917, succeeding another famous character of the same species, 'Brum II', who had been on the job for more than seven years, and who collected more than £1500 for the fund. Among his supporters were King George V and Queen Mary. 'Buller' was on the job for many years, and is well remembered by the present author.

64 North British Railway: The Port Carlisle Dandy.

It was customary for lightly-used branch lines to be worked under the 'one-engine-in-steam' regulations. The principle was, of course, that with only one engine in steam there could be no fear of a collision. From a branch of the North British Railway, that ran from Carlisle westwards to the Solway Firth port of Silloth there was a subsidiary branch from Drumburgh, running for about three miles to Port Carlisle. This also had only one source of motive power; but it was a horse, not a locomotive. The Dandy plied back and forth, but where it entered upon the main branch line at Drumburgh it was signalled as an ordinary train. The Dandy ceased operation in 1911, and its passing was the occasion of much nostalgic sentiment in the district. A post-card was published with the following lines printed over a picture of the Dandy:

'Farewell, farewell our own beloved Dandy,
To children's children ye have faithful been,
Still dear to us and ours, as to our fathers
We sing thy praise to keep thy mem'ry green;

No rush, no roar—ye bore your happy
  cargoes,
With ease and grace that was akin to pride
And tender recollections ever cluster,
Round thee and that fair port by Solway's
  tide;
Farewell, old friend, farewell old times,
  old customs,
Alas, the dear old Dandy's reign is o'er
But in fond hearts that homely horse-
  drawn wagon
Remains a "Coach of State" for evermore!'

65 Hump Shunting in Arabia

The usual understanding of 'hump shunting' is in connection with the mechaniz-
ation of busy marshalling yards and the
propelling of wagons over an artificially
raised 'hump' in the track to give them
impetus to run by gravity into the
appropriate reception sidings. But coming
upon the scene 'somewhere in the Middle
East' depicted in our picture, our friend
the photographer could not help affixing
a title 'hump shunting', and hump shunting
it actually was! It is certainly not the only
instance to be recalled of camels being used
for railway work; but the other one
involved the use of camels in teams,
ploughing to prepare the ground for
track laying across the well-nigh limitless
expanse of the Nullarbor Plain in Australia,
where the country is so devoid of any hills,
rivers, or other physical features as to
enable the Trans-Australian railway to be
laid completely straight for 297 miles!
(See also ref. 170.)

66 Paris–Orléans Railway: The First
'Pacific' Locomotive in Europe.

The Paris–Orléans Railway had followed
the Northern in adopting the De Glehn

system of compounding for its express
passenger locomotives, and some powerful
and efficient 'Atlantics' had formed the
pattern for two similar engines purchased
by the English Great Western Railway for
trial. While the Bordeaux main line of the
Orléans Railway boasted a very straight
alignment, and was not troubled by any
severe gradient, the line to Toulouse was
extremely difficult, and it was for the
very hilly route that runs via Limoges that
these first 'Pacifics' were introduced. The
first engine of the class, No. 4501, was
allocated to Limoges depot when first
put into service in July 1907. These
remarkable engines were De Glehn four-
cylinder compounds, and had coupled
wheels of a smaller diameter (6 ft. 0 in.)
than then usual for express passenger units,
to render them more suitable for climbing
the severe gradients. The cylinder diam-
eters were $15\frac{3}{8}$ in. high pressure, $25\frac{1}{4}$ in.
low pressure, each with a stroke of $25\frac{1}{2}$ in.;
the boiler pressure was 227 lb. per sq. in.,
and the total weight of engine alone in
working order was 89 tons. They were not
superheated. Proving very successful, a
further 68 engines were added to the
initial two built for trial, and a further 30
followed, fitted with superheaters.

67 French Western Railway: Four-
cylinder Compound 'Pacific' Locomotive
of 1908.

The Orléans Railway did not have the
distinction of owning the only 'Pacific'
locomotives in Europe for very long, and
in 1908 the Western Railway introduced
two remarkable engines of this type, built
in the company's own works at Sotteville,
near Rouen. They were designed for
working the heavy express trains between
Paris and Cherbourg, and Paris and Brest,
both routes of which include many severe

gradients where the line crosses deep valleys running towards the sea. These engines, of very striking appearance, due to their greatly extended smokeboxes, had a layout of cylinders that was the reverse of the De Glehn arrangement. The high-pressure cylinders were inside and driving the leading pair of coupled wheels, while the large low-pressure cylinders, and their associated piston valves, were outside, and by their very size contributed to the striking appearance of these engines. The cylinder diameters were $15\frac{3}{4}$ in. high pressure, and 26 in. low pressure, both with a stroke of $25\frac{1}{4}$ in.; the coupled-wheel diameter was 6 ft. $4\frac{1}{2}$ in., and the boiler pressure 235 lb. per sq. in. The engine alone in working order weighed 91 tons, and the large bogie tender a further 57 tons. Shortly after their introduction, however, the Western Railway was absorbed into the State system, and these two very interesting locomotives remained the only ones of their kind.

68 **Paris, Lyons, and Mediterranean Railway:** Four-cylinder Compound 'Pacific' Locomotive of 1909.

The 'P.L.M.', to use the familiar initials of this most famous of French railways, had a long and distinguished history of loco-motive development, and in 1909, to meet the needs for greater power in hauling heavier and more luxurious trains between Paris and the South of France, the company built in its own shops in Paris two 'Pacific' locomotives for trial. These two loco-motives formed the pioneers of a long range of 'Pacifics' of such excellent design and construction that they were capable of many subsequent modernizations and were among the last 'Pacifics' of any kind to remain in service on the French railways

until the late 1960s. It is interesting that one of them, which has been preserved, has been brought to England, and is kept at Carnforth, Lancashire. Our picture shows one of a batch built in 1912, by the German firm of Henschel. The P.L.M. authorities made considerable trials of four-cylinder simple locomotives in com-petition with compounds; but ultimately the verdict was in favour of the compounds. The latter had high-pressure cylinders $17\frac{3}{8}$ in. diameter by $25\frac{5}{8}$ in. stroke, and the low-pressure cylinders had both diameter and stroke of $25\frac{7}{8}$ in. The coupled wheels were 6 ft. $6\frac{3}{4}$ in. diameter, and the boiler pressure 227 lb. per sq. in. With their later developments and modernizations these 'Pacifics' must be regarded as among the most successful express passenger loco-motives ever to run in France.

69 **French State Railways:** De Glehn Four-cylinder Compound 'Pacific' Loco-motive of 1910.

The State Railway System, in developing its locomotive power, adopted the De Glehn form of compound layout in some large 'Pacific' engines introduced in 1910 for the heavy boat express trains between Paris and Le Havre, and Paris and Dieppe. A total of sixty engines of this type was built, by a number of French engineering firms, between 1910 and 1912. Like the pioneer European compounds these État Pacifics had reduced-size coupled wheels, of 6 ft. 0 in. diameter. The cylinder diam-eters were 15 in. high pressure and $26\frac{1}{4}$ in. low pressure, both with a stroke of $25\frac{1}{4}$ in. and the boiler pressure was the usual for French compounds of the day, 227 lb. per sq. in. Despite its large size and ample tractive power this new locomotive was lighter than the majority of its predecessors, weighing no more than 80 tons. The class had what a noted French writer described as 'a great simplicity of line', with the straight running-plate. The right-hand side of the engine, as shown in our picture, had certain accessories hung on, and to British eyes the presence of the sandbox on the top of the boiler, between the chimney and the dome, does not improve the appearance. They did excellent work in service. It is interesting to recall that some of their large bogie tenders were fitted with pick-up water scoops.

70 London and North Western Railway: Lineside Postal Nets.

Conveyance of the Royal Mail in Great Britain by train reached its zenith in the first decade of the twentieth century. The apparatus for picking and setting down mail at speed had been developed to such a degree of perfection that the exchange could be made at speeds up to about 80 m.p.h. To do so without damage to the contents of the mail-bags required an extremely robust apparatus, and the lineside nets, which received the bags from a speeding mail train were designed so as to 'break its fall', as it were. Sometimes there would be a mishap, and a bag might be torn open and its contests strewn along the line; but such occasions were extremely rare. Before the days of road motor vehicles, by which country mail could be distributed, many quite small towns had their mail deliveries made at speed from a non-stopping mail train. Today there are few trains by which mail is collected and set down by 'the apparatus' as it is usually termed; but in the period covered in this book the apparatus at some stations would be worked several times a day, as well as in connection with the principal night mail

trains. There were, prior to the First World War, mail trains with exchanging apparatus on several main routes out of London, as well as on the very important cross-country mails.

71 Swiss Federal Railways: Six-wheeled Mail Van.

Mail traffic was always a priority business in the heyday of railways, and even today, when mail that is consigned across the great oceans of the world, or across the 'narrow seas' around Great Britain is sent by air, the railway mail services in all countries remain very important. In the period covered by this book there was no alternative to the railway on land, and early in the present century the Swiss Post Office laid down specifications for the new type of mail-van illustrated. This was used on what was then no more than partially an international route, working between Portarlier, Lausanne, and Brigue, on the fast-running line beside the Lake of Geneva, and up the valley of the Rhône. At that time the Simplon Tunnel was not in existence, and Brigue was the terminus of the line. Mail proceeding into Italy by that route had to be taken over the hazardous Simplon Pass by road mail coach. It is interesting to find that this relatively modern vehicle was non-bogie. On each side there were large sliding doors to provide ample space for loading and unloading, and the end platforms and side galleries will be noted. The vans were electrically lighted.

72 Prussian State Railways: Bogie Corridor Mail Van.

The inclusion of mail, or travelling post office vans, in express passenger trains usually involves marshalling the mail-vans, either at the extreme front or the extreme rear of the trains. In the ordinary way there is not any communication between the mail and passenger portions of the train. It would in any case be highly undesirable, or even dangerous for the public to have any access to the mail-vans. On the Prussian State Railways in the days before the First World War they did however find the need to provide mail-vans with corridor connections, so that they could be marshalled at an intermediate point in an express train and not prevent communication between front and rear of the train. This Prussian van included store space and the usual sorting accommodation. The corridor ran down one side and was shut off completely from the mail room. Inner doors were provided, and these could be shut across the corridor when the outer doors on that side of the carriage were being used for the receipt or delivery of mails. This would be done only at stations, and the temporary cutting-off of the corridor communication would not cause any inconvenience at such times. The apparatus for picking up and setting down mails at speed was fitted only on one side of the car, as on British T.P.O. vans. In the Prussian case the apparatus was, of course, on the opposite side to the passenger corridor.

73 **London and North Western Railway:** Travelling Post Office, Mail Exchanging Apparatus.

The London and North Western Railway was the principal carrier of mails in England, and with its Scottish partner, the Caledonian, it operated the Royal Mail 'Special'—an exclusively postal train—running between London, Glasgow, Edin-burgh, and Aberdeen. The close-up view of the exchanging apparatus on the mail-van shows the complementary set of equipment to the lineside nets shown under reference 70. The train could not proceed for the whole of the journey with the equipment in the position shown because of the out-stretched net, and bars carrying the mail-bags to be set down would strike the sides of bridges, and other lineside objects. The nets were located at places on the lineside where there was a considerable clear space beforehand, and the postal sorters on the train had to know, without any doubt, the exact moment when the apparatus could be safely extended. In certain places the passage through a station would be the cue; in others one might wait for junction points, then count three over-bridges, and extend the apparatus. It was a matter of split-second timing, often with the train travelling at more than 70 m.p.h. With much of it done in darkness, the men on the apparatus had to know every sound on the line and act like lightning at the correct moment.

74 **Great Western Railway:** Engine Decorated to Haul Funeral Train of King Edward VII in 1910.

The working of royal trains on the British railways had always been the occasion of the utmost precaution, and although the restrictions on speed had been greatly relaxed since the death of Queen Victoria, a funeral train was not the occasion for any fast running. There was even more need for extreme caution with the train conveying the funeral cortège of King Edward VII, in 1910, on its relatively short run from Paddington to Windsor. There had probably never before been such a gathering of European royalty, and there has scarcely been a similar one since. With the exception of France, nearly every country in Europe had its Emperor, or King; though with the First World War some of the greatest of those royal dynasties disappeared. It was commented at the time that the Great Western driver of the engine *King Edward*, draped in purple for the occasion, had an incredible responsibility. A slip on his part, and half Europe could be plunged in mourning, and the most incalculable political situations set up. The engine in question was one of the famous 'Star' class, of four-cylinder 4-6-0s.

75   Great Indian Peninsular Railway: 4-4-0 Express Passenger Engine Decorated for Royal Train Workings.

The great Imperial Durbar of 1911 staged to celebrate the accession to the throne of King George V, Emperor of India, involved the running of many special trains, both for the British royalty visiting India on that grand occasion and for other high dignitaries. The Bengal Nagpur, the Bombay, Baroda and Central India, the East Indian, and the Great Indian Peninsula Railways were all involved. Each had their own distinctive liveries, of green, black, red-brown, and chocolate respectively, but a specially heavy burden of Royal Train workings fell upon the G.I.P.R., and for the occasion the railway departed from its standard livery, and finished all the engines concerned in a magnificent special style depicted in our illustration. No fewer than thirteen engines were so treated: four 4-4-0s, as in our picture; two 4-6-0s; five 'Atlantics', and even two of the huge 2-8-4 tank engines used exclusively for banking on the Ghat inclines. All except the latter were named specially after members of the Royal Family, including some

then deceased as, for example, *Edward VII*, *Queen Victoria*, and *Prince Albert*. The magnificent array of flags, together with the royal arms was carried on the locomotives hauling the King Emperor himself.

76   Midland Railway: 4-4-0 Express Locomotive Prepared for the Royal Train.

There was considerable difference in the way the various railway companies dealt with royal specials. The London and North Western, which in conveyance of the King and Queen to Balmoral had some of the longest mileages to perform did not decorate its engines at all. Even for so special occasion as the Investiture of the Prince of Wales, at Carnarvon, in 1912, the locomotives concerned were quite unadorned, albeit specially selected units. The Midland Railway did not often have the task of working royal trains, but the engine illustrated shows a form of adornment that is, so far as is known, unique. It was one of the standard Class '2' 4-4-0 superheater locomotives, but on this occasion its identity was suppressed. The number was removed from the smokebox door, and the customary large figures on the tender painted out. Instead, the Royal Cipher was embellished on the cab side, specially for the occasion. The finish of Midland passenger engines in the period under review was always immaculate, and one can well imagine how this specially prepared engine appeared on 'the day'. It was actually engine No. 502.

77   London, Brighton, and South Coast Railway: 4-4-2 Tank Engine Decorated for the Royal Train.

This engine was also prepared for conveyance of King Edward VII, though a happier occasion than that of the Great

Western engine (ref. 74). It was Derby Day, and the King and his party travelled from Victoria Station, London, to Epsom. The Brighton railway honoured the festive occasion by splendidly decorating the engine, though from all accounts the journeys gave the responsible railway officers some anxiety. This time it was not any fear of wrecking, or any other dire calamity, but simply the steaming capacity of the engine! D. Earle Marsh's 4–4–2 tank engines were the last word in Brighton suburban power at the time, and in 1907 one of the 'I1' class had given much trouble in working the Royal Train up the steep gradients leading up to Epsom. In 1908 one of the larger 'I2' class was put on, and it is this engine that is illustrated. Although not one of the most *puissant* of the Brighton engines, with skilful handling she managed the Royal Train successfully. The cylinders were only $17\frac{1}{2}$ in. diameter by 26 in. stroke; the boiler and firebox were very small, and the boiler pressure 170 lb. per sq. in.

78 **Great Northern Railway:** 40-ton Bogie Well Wagon, Carrying Locomotive.

This rather striking picture has been prepared from a photograph taken in Doncaster works yard. The bogie well wagon was designed for carrying a load up to 40 tons, and the novel idea was formed of testing it, after manufacture, in carrying a complete locomotive. It will be appreciated from a study of this picture that although the 'well' portion of the wagon is as low as practicable the locomotive mounted on it would be too tall to clear the loading gauge, because the chimney extends practically to the limit when the locomotive is standing on the track in the ordinary way. Sometimes when it has been necessary to transport non-operable locomotives the chimney and dome cover has been temporarily removed. In the ordinary way, of course, a locomotive would be moved from one part of the line to another under its own steam. The engine in question is one of the famous Stirling 8-foot bogie singles, slightly modernized by H. A. Ivatt, by fitting a domed boiler. The wagon itself has a body consisting of four parallel steel-plate girders substantially braced together and carried on the so-called diamond-framed bogies. The kind of load for which wagons of this kind were used to convey, in revenue-earning service can be seen under reference 12, in which a wagon of Great Central design is transporting a huge boiler.

79 **Great Northern Railway:** 20-ton Eight-wheeled Goods Brake Van.

The old traditional practice of running loose-coupled freight trains on British Railways with no brake power other than that provided by the locomotive and the brake van has several times been commented upon, particularly under reference 7. This had other implications beside that of locomotive power. The brake, or guard's van, at the rear end had a most important function to perform, particularly on sections of line where there were lengthy gradients. The driver and guard, working with a perfect understanding, had to operate the locomotive and brake on the rear van so as to keep the train running at a speed from which it could be readily stopped, if required. This, on even a moderate gradient, would be quite slow. The Great Northern Railway used to operate some of the heaviest freight trains in Great Britain between Peterborough and London, the coal trains frequently exceeding a total load, behind the tender of 1200 tons. The special eight-wheeled brake vans were specially designed for working on these very heavy trains. They were the only eight-wheeled non-bogie brake vans ever to run in Great Britain. Their braking power was considerably greater than that of various 20-ton vans on other railways having four or six wheels, because the screw-brake was provided with an equalizing gear to apply the power simultaneously through sixteen brake blocks.

80 **Great Northern Railway:** 35-ton Open Bogie Wagon used for Brick Traffic.

While the familiar four-wheeled wagon, either open or closed, was by far the commonest and most popular for general freight traffic in Great Britain, attention has already been drawn in this book to a number of special types introduced for special traffic. It was not always easy to do this, because sidings and yard accommodation both on the railways themselves and in factories and other traders' premises beside the line had developed to deal only with the four-wheeled wagon. On the belt of clay lying just to the south of Peterborough extensive brickworks developed. The bricks were needed in the London district in large quantities, and the Great Northern Railway made special arrangements to deal with this profitable traffic expeditiously. There was no difficulty in dealing with large wagons in the new sidings laid alongside the line between Yaxley and Fletton, and the long bogie wagons illustrated were designed for each to convey 35 tons of bricks. The fully loaded weight of each was $49\frac{1}{2}$ tons, and a train of twenty or more of them would be

worked up to London in the same style as the heavy coal trains, using the eight-wheeled brake vans (ref. 79) when available.

81 **London Brighton and South Coast Railway:** Inspection Saloon.

Among railway carriages built other than for public use, inspection saloons usually have many interesting features. In 1914 the beautiful vehicle illustrated was completed at the Lancing Works of the L.B. & S.C.R. for the use of directors and principal officers. To give a complete outlook over the track when running the observation ends of the saloon were made in bay-window form. Inside there were two principal compartments, 12 ft. and 26 ft. long respectively. They were connected by a corridor which also gave access to a lavatory and butler's pantry. The small compartment was equipped with lounge-type chairs, while the large one had tables that could be used for conference or board meetings, or alternatively for dining. The chairs in the compartment were of the small dining-room type. The saloon itself was 60 ft. long and was notable in two respects that apart from the Pullman cars it was the only twelve-wheeled carriage to be operated by the L.B. & S.C.R.; it also carried the crest of the company, which was carried only on a very few express passenger locomotives. It would be incorrect to say it was the only twelve-wheeled carriage to run on this railway, because on the famous 'Sunny South Special' between Eastbourne, Brighton, Liverpool, and Manchester, the London and North Western Railway provided the stock, and included in these trains were the familiar L.N.W.R. twelve-wheeled dining-cars.

82 **The Maharajah of Rewar:** Saloon Car in his Private Train.

In the days of the Indian Empire, many native princes had their own trains which they used when travelling not only in their own domains but further afield in India. A remarkable example of these was that used by the Maharajah of Rewar. It consisted of six coaches, four of which were four-wheelers for use of the staff, while two highly fanciful saloons were provided for the Maharajah and the Maharanee. As will be appreciated from this picture the appearance was striking, to say the least of it. The companion saloon was originally striped in the style of a tiger's coat, but was later changed to a highly coloured imitation of marble! The car illustrated was built to the full size permitted by the Indian broad gauge; but the 'marble' car, which was 43 ft. long, against the 66 ft. of the one illustrated, was so designed that it could be adapted to run over metre-gauge lines. The body could be lifted from the broad-gauge bogies, and lowered on to metre-gauge ones when required. This was at one time quite a common provision on State carriages in India. The striking appearance of the complete train was set off by the smart finish of the four-wheeled end carriages, which were painted in bright yellow, and had the once-typical sunshades over the windows.

83 **London and North Western Railway:** Observation Car on Scenic North Wales Routes.

The London and North Western Railway had some most picturesque routes on both its main lines and branch lines in North Wales. The far-famed Chester and Holyhead line, the route of the Irish Mail, skirted the beautiful coast between Prestatyn and Bangor, threading the great headlands by tunnel and often running on viaducts virtually in the sea. But the heaviness of the traffic on this route precluded the making of any special arrangements for sightseeing, and it was on the single-line branch running southwards from Llandudno Junction to Blaenau Ffestiniog that a splendidly equipped observation car was run, from 1911 onwards, specially for tourist sightseeing. It was attached to the rear of a branch-line train, and for a very small extra charge passengers could travel in this beautiful car, which was almost 'all windows'. A pleasant, and very knowledgeable guide travelled in the car, and pointed out features of interest along the line. These included many delightful stretches of the River Conway, and distant views of Snowdon. On the return journey the car was detached from the train at Bettws-y-coed to give time for a short tour of the beautiful river scenery in the neighbourhood. The car was then attached to a later train for the completion of the journey back to Llandudno.

84 **South Eastern and Chatham Railway:** Post Office Sorting Van.

In these days, when such a high proportion of mail leaving Great Britain goes by air, it is perhaps a little difficult to appreciate something of the working conditions when everything went by train and boat. The South Eastern and Chatham Railway not only handled a heavy mail traffic between England and the continent of Europe, but also took a share in the working of the celebrated Imperial Indian mail. To save time on the journey this was conveyed overland from Calais, through France and Italy, to catch the steamer at Brindisi, and the S.E. & C.R. provided the link between London and Dover. The mail-vans illustrated were introduced for these important services and were interesting in carrying the inscription *Malle Royale* in addition to *Royal Mail*. The daily morning continental mail train from Cannon Street to Dover usually had at least three of these vans. They had vestibule connections, so that the entire mail portions of the train were in communication, and internal arrangements for the sorting of mail were designed specially for the various services operated. They were also used on the 'Dover Mail', that catered for inland mail traffic between south-eastern England and London. None of the S.E. & C.R. travelling post office vans were fitted with apparatus for exchange of mail-bags without stopping.

85 **Johore State Railway:** 'Pacific' Type Express Passenger Locomotive.

The opening of this railway, in 1909, provided the last link, 100 miles long, in the chain of railway communication between Penang and Singapore, though actually the railway termini at each end were on the mainland immediately opposite the ferries plying to the islands of Penang and Singapore. Railway construction had proceeded independently at first in the States eventually grouped in the Malayan Federation, but by the early years of the present century unification of railways into the Federated Malay States system was an accomplished fact. The construction of the final link, through Johore, was accompanied by a certain display of individuality; for although all States involved in the running of the Penang–

Singapore through service used the same design of 'Pacific' locomotive those operating in Johore were painted a distinctive livery. The standard colour on the F.M.S.R. was light green, but the Johore State Railway adopted the splendid dark blue of the Caledonian Railway, with its handsome accompaniment of claret-coloured under-frames. Although of the 'Pacific' type, these engines were small by British and continental standards. The two cylinders were $15\frac{1}{2}$ in. diameter by 24 in. stroke; coupled wheels 4 ft. 6 in. The total weight of engine and tender in working order was only 76 tons.

86 **San Paulo Railway (Brazil):** 'Pacific' Type Express Passenger Locomotive.

In some contrast to the Johore 'Pacific' locomotive illustrated on the same page, the San Paulo engine is a large and powerful type designed for heavy working on the 5 ft. 3 in. gauge. Though not intended for really fast running, in the style of contemporary British and French services, these engines, which were built by the North British Locomotive Company, were designed for the highest-class passenger service then offered in South America. The San Paulo was then British-owned, and the appearance and technical details of these 'Pacifics' were essentially British, with such decorative features as polished brass domes, and caps to the chimneys, and the typical shape of safety-valve cover. An interesting feature is the provision of two entirely separate safety-valves abreast of each other. While double safety-valves were becoming quite common in England at the time they were usually mounted within a single large casing. These engines had two cylinders $21\frac{1}{2}$ in. diameter by 26 in. stroke;

coupled wheels of 5 ft. 6 in. diameter, and a boiler pressure of 200 lb. per sq. in. The Schmidt superheater was used, together with Dr Schmidt's patent design of piston valves. The total weight of engine and tender in working order was 118·4 tons.

87 Egyptian State Railways: Superheated 'Atlantic' Type Express Locomotive.

The operating conditions on the Egyptian State Railways are more difficult than perhaps might be appreciated. Although the country is mainly level the climate of Egypt is tropical and at times the prevailing winds are very strong, and lead to severe sand-storms. The specification laid down for the new 'Atlantic' locomotives illustrated was a severe one. In any conditions of weather, cross-winds or not, they were required to maintain a speed of 60 m.p.h. on straight level track with a load of 450 tons. Furthermore, as some of the yards include sharp turnouts and curves, a degree of flexibility in wheelbase was demanded. The Berlin Locomotive Works secured the order, and the engines were delivered at Alexandria at the end of 1913. They had two cylinders 20 in. diameter by 26 in. stroke; coupled wheels 6 ft. 6 in. diameter; a very large boiler and superheater provided a combined total heating surface of 2616 sq. ft., and a grate area of 30·9 sq. ft. The boiler pressure was 180 lb. per sq. in. The valve gear was Walschaerts. The total weight of engine in working order was 73 tons, and of the large bogie tender 65 tons. The latter was provided to permit of non-stop running over the 130 miles between Cairo and Alexandria. The designer was Mr R. G. Peckitt, Chief

Mechanical Engineer of the Egyptian State Railways.

88 Northern Railway of France: Four-cylinder Compound 'Pacific' Locomotive (De Glehn System).

Under reference 153 the circumstances that led to the development of the great new 4–6–4 compound express locomotives not being proceeded with are described. Instead the Nord, somewhat hurriedly, followed the trend of affairs elsewhere in France, and adopted the 'Pacific' type. It so happened that Mr De Glehn's firm, the Société Alsacienne of Belfort, had recently delivered some Pacific locomotives to the Alsace-Lorraine Railways, and the design adopted by the Nord was practically the same. The fact that a railway previously famed for such individuality and prowess as the Nord did this is enough to show the urgency of the situation. The second point to be noted is that in that period, between 1871 and the outbreak of the First World War, the French provinces of Alsace and Lorraine were part of the German Empire, and their railways had been extensively Germanized. Nevertheless, the Société Alsacienne, although situated in Belfort, had rendered immense assistance to the development of French locomotive practice. The new Nord 'Pacifics', of which a first batch of twenty were delivered in 1912, had a cylinder diameter of $16\frac{3}{8}$ in. high pressure and $23\frac{5}{8}$ in. low pressure, each with a stroke of $26\frac{3}{8}$ in. The coupled-wheel diameter was 6 ft. $8\frac{1}{2}$ in., and the boiler pressure 227 lb. per sq. in. The weight of engine alone, in working order, was 85 tons. They did some excellent work with the heavy and fast English boat trains, between Paris and Calais, and Paris and Boulogne.

89 Lancashire and Yorkshire Railway: 4-4-0 Superheated Express Passenger Locomotive.

Many factors towards the improvement of locomotive performance were being studied at the Horwich Works of the Lancashire and Yorkshire Railway in the 1900-10 period. Extensive experiments were being made with compounding, and at the same time trials were in progress with the use of superheated steam. In 1909 four express passenger locomotives of the very successful Aspinall 4-4-0 class, with 7 ft. 3 in. coupled wheels, were taken and rebuilt with larger boilers, super-heaters providing a much higher steam temperature, and a general reconstruction that completely altered the look of the engines. More important still, however, was a redesign of the cylinders and valve gear, which gave an extremely free flow of steam, and produced an exceedingly fast-running engine. These rebuilt locomotives were frequently employed on the fast lightly-loaded business expresses running between Manchester and Liverpool in 40 minutes. Speeds up to 85 m.p.h. were attained on favourable stretches of the line. The curious thing was that on the Lancashire and Yorkshire Railway the factors that had contributed to the success of these engines was not at once appreciated, and it was not until many years later that their extreme significance was generally appreciated.

90 North Eastern Railway: 4-4-4 Three-cylinder Express Tank Engine.

The North Eastern Railway, with its virtual monopoly of traffic in England north of the Humber, had many centres from which fast passenger services were being developed, and the use of express passenger locomotives that had been superseded on the principal main-line duties was not entirely satisfactory. Vincent L. Raven, the Chief Mechanical Engineer, therefore applied the three-cylinder system of propulsion, which had proved very successful on his large main-line engines, to a fast and powerful tank engine designed on the most modern lines, and which could be used on residential services radiating from Leeds, Newcastle, Hull, and other large centres of population. He used the 4-4-4 wheel arrangement, so that the engines could be run with equal facility in either direction. There would be no need to turn them at the outer terminal stations. First introduced in 1913 these engines were very successful, and a further batch of them was built after the First World War. In later years, when the loading of fast local trains increased, largely through the introduction of improved coaching stock, with greater amenities, it was found necessary to increase the adhesion weight of these engines, and they were converted from the 4-4-4 to the 4-6-2 type.

91 North British Railway: The REID 'Atlantic' Express Passenger Engine.

In 1906, when larger locomotives were needed for the highly competitive services from Edinburgh and Glasgow to Aberdeen, and also for the Anglo-Scottish services via the Midland route, which the North British operated between Edinburgh and Carlisle, some surprise was expressed that for these heavily graded routes the 'Atlantic' type was chosen in preference to the 4-6-0. But the REID 'Atlantics', particularly after they were equipped with superheaters, were extremely competent engines. They were capable of a high output of power on heavy gradients; they were not susceptible to slipping and they had a long record of most reliable service. They were all distinguished by fine Scottish names, appropriate to the routes over which they ran, such as *Aberdonian*, *Bonnie Dundee*, *Thane of Fife*, and the one shown in our picture *Cock o'the North*. Those working on the route to Carlisle included *Hazeldean*, *Abbotsford*, *Teribus*, *Waverley*, and *Borderer*. Our picture shows the original North British bronze-green livery. After the grouping of the railways in 1923 they were painted in the standard 'apple-green' style of the L.N.E.R. and if anything looked still finer. After a life of strenuous work they were withdrawn from service in the late 1930s. The name *Cock o'the North* was used on the first of Sir Nigel Gresley's 2–8–2 engines, in 1934.

92 Netherlands State Railways: Four-cylinder 4–6–0 Express Passenger Locomotive.

Under reference 19, an interesting 4–6–0 express passenger locomotive for the Netherlands Central Railway was illustrated and described, and its typically German characteristics mentioned. At about the same time the State Railway was also taking delivery of some 4–6–0s which were four-cylinder simples, but which were British built, by Beyer, Peacock & Co. Ltd. This firm had been suppliers of locomotives to Holland for many years previously, and the new 4–6–0s were essentially British in appearance, with a low running-plate, and a minimum of 'works' outside. The valve gear was Walschaerts but arranged inside, and the valves of the outside cylinders were actuated through rocking levers. The only feature that marred the appearance of these otherwise

extremely handsome locomotives was the height of the chimney, which seemed disproportionately tall in respect of the other boiler mountings. They were designed for heavy pulling rather than high speed, because the maximum permitted anywhere on the system was 56 m.p.h. The heavy international express trains were allowed 54 minutes to cover the 35 miles between Utrecht and Arnhem. The four cylinders were $15\frac{3}{4}$ in. diameter by 26 in. stroke; coupled wheels were 6 ft. 1 in. diameter, and the boiler pressure 170 lb. per sq. in. The boilers were large, and equipped with high-degree superheating. They proved most successful, and for many years formed the standard passenger class on the State Railways.

93 Swedish State Railways: Superheated 'Atlantic' Type Express Locomotive.

The railways of Scandinavia, taken collectively, favoured outside cylinders for all locomotives, whether for passenger, goods, or local services, and it is therefore interesting to find this very striking express locomotive of 1908 with inside cylinders. There are certain very distinctive features about this design. The running-plate is carried very high, completely clear of the coupled wheels, and at the same time providing a better access to the inside machinery. To provide as much space as possible for the inside cylinders, valve gear, and associated equipment the leading bogie has been designed with outside frames, while the engine main frames are splayed outwards at the leading end to give maximum space between. By contemporary standards it was not a large engine, having cylinders $19\frac{11}{16}$ in.

diameter by $23\frac{5}{8}$ in. stroke; coupled wheels 6 ft. 2 in. diameter, and a boiler pressure of 170 lb. per sq. in. A high degree of superheat in the steam was aimed at, as the superheater was large in relation to the evaporative heating surface of the boiler: 353 sq. ft. against 1432 sq. ft. An important external feature in a country experiencing such extremes of winter weather as Sweden, is the very commodious and well-protected cab, with back shields on the tender.

94 **Norwegian State Railways:** 2–8–0 Freight Engine, built in the U.S.A., 1919.

Railway operating conditions in Norway are exceptionally severe. Not only are all lines subject to extremes of climate, with long months of very little daylight in the winter to add to the almost perpetual ice and snow in that season, but in crossing the mountain ranges very heavy gradients are encountered. Furthermore, it is an astonishing fact that nearly two-thirds of the entire area of the country is untillable, consisting of rock areas and mountains, many of which are covered with eternal snow and ice. Yet it was essential to connect the scattered and important centres of population, and from an early date the majority of the railways became owned by the State, and were operated as an essential, if not necessarily economic service. Having little in the way of heavy industry in the country locomotives and equipment generally were imported, and during the First World War this led to a difficult situation, when most of the normal suppliers in Europe were belligerents on one side or the other. Locomotives had, however, been obtained from the U.S.A. at intervals since the year 1879, and

it was to the firm of Baldwins that the Norwegian State Railways turned when additional locomotives were needed in 1916–18. The engine shown in our picture was one of a new design put into service in 1919. Unlike most previous supplies from the U.S.A., which were of standard American designs readily adapted to Norwegian conditions, the new 2–8–0s were of entirely Norwegian design, in a new, indigenous style of outline, yet nevertheless conforming to current American ideas. The two cylinders were $22\frac{1}{2}$ in. diameter by $25\frac{1}{4}$ in. stroke; the coupled wheels were 4 ft. $1\frac{1}{4}$ in. diameter, and the boiler pressure 170 lb. per sq. in. The weight of engine alone in working order was $64\frac{1}{4}$ tons. The completely closed-in cab was a new feature, well suited to working in a severe climate.

95 **Norwegian State Railways:** 2–6–2 Suburban Passenger Tank Engine.

Included in the programme of modernization, with indigenous Norwegian designs, was an interesting series of tank engines, the first of which took the road in 1916. This was an 0–10–0 for yard shunting work, and was one of the first American-built locomotives in Norway to depart from the typical American 'look'. Two of these engines were supplied by Baldwins, and three others in clearly the same style of external design were built for short-haul freight working, also in 1916. These latter engines were of the 2–8–2 type. Then in 1919 came the very handsome 2–6–2 passenger tank engine illustrated, one of a batch of seven. These most distinctive little engines had cylinders $20\frac{1}{2}$ in. diameter by $23\frac{5}{8}$ in. stroke; coupled wheels 5 ft. 3 in. diameter, and a boiler pressure of 170 lb.

per sq. in. The total engine weight was $65\frac{1}{2}$ tons in working order.

96 Danish State Railways: Three-cylinder 4–6–0 Superheated Express Passenger Locomotive.

The geography of Denmark precludes anything in the way of long-distance express running, such as was currently being performed in Great Britain, France, and America, and to a lesser degree, and at somewhat lower speeds, in Germany. But the Danish railways have always been very smartly run, and in providing motive power for expresses in connection with the Harwich steamer services to Esbjerg, and other runs in Jutland, they owned a notable collection of steam locomotives in an interesting variety of types. Heavy industry in Denmark having developed slowly the great majority of the locomotives had been purchased elsewhere, and until the year 1924 mainly from Germany. In the years before the First World War the firm of A. Borsig, with works at Tegel, on the outskirts of Berlin, had indulged in a notable 'tidying up' of the outlines of their locomotives, in a style that was sometimes referred to as 'Imitation British'! Of this there could be no more striking example than the Servian 0–10–0 (ref. 133). The fine 4–6–0 express locomotive illustrated, which dates from 1913, is definitely continental, in the high-raised running-plate exposing driving wheels and motion, but the boiler mountings are conspicuously neat. The three cylinders, all driving on the leading pair of coupled wheels, were $18\frac{1}{2}$ in. diameter by $26\frac{1}{2}$ in. stroke; the coupled wheels diameter was 6 ft. $1\frac{1}{2}$ in., and the boiler pressure 170 lb. per sq. in. Further locomotives of the same type were added after the First World War, but built in Denmark, at the Frich Works in Aarhus.

97 Swiss Federal Railways: Two-cylinder Compound 4–4–0 Express Locomotive.

The railways of Switzerland are famed for the dramatic way in which many of the main routes have been engineered through the tremendous mountain fastnesses of the Alps; but on the other hand there are several important main lines following some of the great river valleys, or in less mountainous country that have comparatively easy gradients and permit of fast running. On these routes many of the principal express trains were hauled by 4–4–0 locomotives. In accordance with general European preferences in the 1900–10 period these engines were compounds having two cylinders inside. They had a neat appearance more in keeping with contemporary British and Dutch locomotive practice, though including certain distinctive features. The cylinder diameters were 18 in. high pressure, and $26\frac{3}{4}$ in. low pressure, with a common stroke of 26 in.; the coupled-wheel diameter was 6 ft. and the boiler pressure 190 lb. per sq. in. The valve gear was Walschaerts, arranged inside, but with the outside return crank mounted on the driving wheel coupling-rod pin. The small snow shields in front of the bogie wheels will be noted, and a characteristic feature was the indicating pointer on the side of the tender showing the extent to which the water tanks were full. These engines worked mostly from Zürich, northwards to Basle; on the line that leads to Austria via Sargans, and on the fast-running main line between Zürich and Lucerne.

98 **Madras Railway:** 4–4–0 Express Passenger and Mail Engine.

During the earlier period covered by this volume the future of the Madras Railway was very much in the balance. It was one of the oldest railways in India, having been opened in 1856, and it was expected that it would be taken over by the Government, and probably amalgamated with other lines already in State ownership. In the event it was amalgamated to form the Madras and South Mahratta system. As an independent concern it formed part of the trunk line across the Indian peninsula connecting Bombay with Madras. Of this very important strategic and mail route, 794 miles long, 351 miles were under the Madras Railway ownership, the rest belonging to the Great Indian Peninsula Railway. The mail trains were hauled by the smart 4–4–0 locomotives shown in our picture. These operated, of course, on the Indian broad gauge of 5 ft. 6 in., although the Madras Railway had, in addition to its 1470 miles of broad gauge 80 miles of metre-gauge line, and a further 43 miles on the 2 ft. 6 in. gauge. The route of the Bombay mails was by no means an easy one. On the eastbound run Raichur, where the Madras Railway took over from the G.I.P.R., was left at 2.56 p.m. and Madras reached at 6 a.m. next morning. This does not suggest very fast running over this 351 miles; but there were many intermediate stops.

99 **Great Northern Railway (Ireland):** Superheated 4–4–0 Express Locomotive.

The Great Northern Railway of Ireland, with its principal main line connecting Dublin with Belfast, was always a system of the first importance, and after the establishment of the Irish Free State it became an international main line. The locomotive works are situated at Dundalk, approximately half-way between the two terminal cities. The main line, over which locomotives worked through without change, includes a variety of running conditions. Between Dublin and Dundalk the gradients are undulating, but not difficult, and the same applies between Portadown and Belfast. Intermediately there is some hard climbing up to Adavoyle summit. Except for some extensive reverse curvature between Goraghwood and Portadown the alignment is good throughout, and with excellent standards of permanent way maintenance some high-speed running was regularly made. The engine illustrated in our picture was one of an enlarged class introduced in 1913; it generally followed the practice of early designs, but was enlarged and included the modern improvement of superheating. The cylinders were 19 in. diameter by 26 in. stroke; coupled wheels 6 ft. 7 in. diameter, and a boiler pressure of 165 lb. per sq. in. The total weight of engine and tender in working order was 82·6 tons. The five engines of the class were named after high mountains in the district served by the Great Northern Railway of Ireland.

100 **Midland Railway (Northern Counties Committee):** 4–4–0 Superheated Express Locomotive.

From the year 1876, when he himself was no more than twenty-two years of age, Mr Bowman Malcolm had been locomotive superintendent at Belfast. At that time it was the Belfast and Northern Counties Railway; but he continued in office for many years after the Midland Railway of England had acquired a controlling influence. For more than thirty years locomotives on the line had been two-cylinder compounds with inside cylinders on the Worsdell von Borries system. So well did these engines perform that some of them were still at work as compounds in the 1930s. With the advent of superheating, however, Bowman Malcolm turned to simple propulsion, and in 1914 some new 4-4-0 express locomotives were built at the works of the English parent company at Derby. There were nevertheless little or no signs of Midland Railway influence. The former rich dark-green livery of the Belfast and Northern Counties Railway had by that time been changed to what was called 'invisible green'. It lasted well, for some locomotives were still carrying it in the mid-1930s, long after the standard livery of the N.C.C. had been changed to Midland red. The new 4-4-0s of 1914 had cylinders 19 in. diameter by 24 in. stroke; coupled wheels 6 ft. 0 in. diameter, and a boiler pressure of 170 lb. per sq. in. The total weight of engine only in working order was 47·6 tons, and of the tender 29·2 tons.

101 Victorian Railways: the 'A2' Class 4-6-0 Express Passenger Locomotive.

Until the year 1907 locomotive design on the Victorian Railways had been very largely a blend of broad specifications laid down by Australian engineers, and the recommendations of manufacturers, mostly English. But the 'A2' 4-6-0, built at Newport Works, near Melbourne, was a completely Australian achievement from the first lines on the drawing-board to the finished product. A splendid job it was too—as near as possible right and free from teething troubles from the very outset. So successful indeed was the pioneer engine that 124 more were built

between 1908 and 1915. These original engines had Stephenson's link motion, but our picture shows the later variety with Walschaerts valve gear. Of these latter sixty were built, production ceasing in 1922. These 185 engines—125 of the earlier variety and 60 of the later were so soundly constructed as to be capable of successive improvements that greatly enhanced their performance. It cannot, however, be said that their appearance was also improved, for the painting became plain, unlined black; the beautifully shaped chimneys were replaced by plain stovepipes, and large smokebox deflectors were fitted on either side of the smokebox. Nevertheless, 'handsome is as handsome does' and the modernized 'A2' 4-6-0s put in a great deal of very hard work. Engine No. 995 of this class is preserved and on display at the Railway Museum, North Williamstown, near Melbourne. The leading dimensions were: cylinders 22 in. diameter by 26 in. stroke; coupled-wheel diameter 6 ft. 1 in.; boiler pressure 185 lb. per sq. in.; tractive effort 27,480 lb.

102 Chinese Government Railways: 'Atlantic' Express Locomotive for the Taokow–Chingua Line.

If a competition were to be held for the most handsome locomotive ever exported from Great Britain one could well imagine that these Chinese 'Atlantics' would come well within the 'top ten'. Their lines have all the grace of British locomotive practice at its most elegant, and the enormous headlight does little or nothing to detract from this appearance. They were designed by Mr Donald Fraser, Locomotive Superintendent of the railway, and built by Kerr, Stuart & Co. of Stoke-on-Trent, in 1912. The leading dimensions indicate no more than a moderate-powered unit, with cylinders 19 in. diameter by 24 in. stroke; coupled wheels 6 ft. o in. diameter, and a boiler pressure of 180 lb. per sq. in. The piston valves, actuated by Stephenson's link motion between the frames, were however large in relation to the size of the cylinders and would ensure a free flow of steam to provide high-power output. The boiler was large, with an exceptionally large grate area for such an engine of 35 sq. ft. They were not superheated engines. The headlight was lit by acetylene gas.

103 **New Zealand Government Railways:** The 'Ab' Class Express Passenger 'Pacific' Locomotive.

In the earlier volume of this series of books, dealing with *Railways at the Zenith of Steam*, this very famous class, although dating from 1915, was included in the 1920–40 coverage because of its predominating part in New Zealand passenger working for many years. In that volume the 'Ab' was illustrated in its later form, with modified headlight and stove-pipe chimney. Our present picture shows the class as originally turned out at the Addington Workshops. In its later form the Westinghouse brake pump was moved from its position on the side of the smokebox to one just ahead of the firebox—still on the left-hand side of the engine. Their introduction during the difficult period of the First World War created a most favourable impression in the locomotive world, and from the original 18 built, in New Zealand in 1915–17, a further 48 were built by the North British Locomotive Company, in Glasgow, in 1921–2, and a further 40 in New Zealand, half in railway shops, and the remainder by A. & G.

Price. An infallible testimony to the excellency of their design was the freedom with which they attained speeds of around 60 m.p.h. (on 3 ft. 6 in. gauge) despite coupled wheels no larger than 4 ft. 6 in. diameter. The two cylinders were 17 in. diameter by 26 in. stroke, and the boiler pressure 180 lb. per sq. in. The tractive effort was 20,000 lb. An unusual feature at the time was the adoption of the Vanderbilt type of tender, of American origin. The 'Ab' was certainly an outstanding design, and remained little changed from its original form during its long life. Scrapping of them did not begin until 1956.

104 **Victorian Railways:** The 'C' Class Heavy Freight 2–8–0.

The success of the 'A2' class 4–6–0 express passenger engines (ref. 101), led to the working out of a companion design for heavy freight working. Its production was delayed somewhat by war conditions, but in 1918 the first of the new class was completed at Newport Works—at that time the heaviest and most powerful steam locomotive in Australia. For a goods locomotive also it was extremely handsome, finished in the fine crimson lake livery with a stylishly shaped chimney and fully lined out, as shown in our picture. After extensive trials 25 further engines of the class were built between 1921 and 1926. They were not among the most numerous of Victorian locomotives but they were very successful, and for an eight-coupled design, with driving wheels of not more than 5 ft. 1 in. diameter, they had a fine turn of speed, running regularly up to 60 m.p.h. Their cylinders were the same as those of the 'A2' 4–6–0s; but with a boiler pressure of 200 lb. per sq. in. their tractive effort was 38,400 lb.—very powerful engines. One of them is preserved and on display in the museum at North Williamstown, but in the later painting style of plain black, with stovepipe chimney, and with the unsightly, yet effective half-height smoke-deflecting plates.

105 **Lehigh and New England Railroad:** A 2–8–0 Freight Locomotive of 1911.

No miscellany of American locomotives would be complete without the inclusion of further examples of the famous 'Mother Hubbard' type, so called from the positioning of the driver in a 'cupboard' mounted astride the boiler. The original idea behind this extraordinary form of construction was to place the driver well forward, where his lookout ahead would not be obscured by smoke beating down. One can appreciate that there was good reason for doing this on a high-speed express passenger locomotive, but 'Mother Hubbards' of all kinds were built for freight, and local commuter services. The Lehigh and New England made extensive use of them, and engines of this kind were built down to the year 1915. The system has been described as a 'belt' railroad, for while much traffic originated in its own somewhat restricted territory it had immediate connections with nine of the larger systems, including the Pennsylvania, New York Central, Erie, Lehigh Valley, and the Reading. The 2–8–0 illustrated was officially described as a 'light' type. It had two cylinders 19 in. diameter by 26 in. stroke; coupled wheels 4 ft. 2 in. diameter, and a boiler pressure of 200 lb. per sq. in. The tractive effort was 32,000 lb. and the total weight of engine only in working order was 65½ tons.

106 **Southern Pacific Railroad:** Cab-in-front Mallet compound 2–8–8–2.

It is perhaps a little difficult, particularly for European readers, to associate railroading in California with severe weather conditions, and the necessity for carrying lengthy stretches in line in mountain territory in snow-sheds, to protect trains from avalanches. Yet it was conditions of this kind that led first of all to the introduction of the Mallet type of articulated locomotive on the Southern Pacific lines. In single-line tunnels, and the lengthy snow-sheds the conditions in the cabs, and the visibility of the line ahead were so often made very difficult by smoke and exhaust steam that the suggestion was made of putting the cabs in front. As oil firing was used no difficulty was experienced in conveying it from the tender, and in 1912 the first examples of the class illustrated were delivered by Baldwins. They were the first American locomotives to have the 2–8–8–2 wheel arrangement, and eventually there were 49 engines of the class. They proved the forerunners of many more 'cab-in-front' Mallets. This earliest class were compounds. The high-pressure cylinders, 26 in. diameter by 30 in. stroke, were beneath the centre of the boiler, and the low pressure, with the huge diameter of 40 in. adjacent to the smokebox. The coupled wheels were 4 ft. 9 in. diameter; the boiler pressure was 200 lb. per sq. in. The engine alone weighed 195 tons in working order.

107 **Pennsylvania Railroad:** The L1s, 2–8–2 Heavy Freight Locomotives.

The Pennsylvania, which was generally considered to be the premier railroad of the U.S.A., was for the most part strictly orthodox in its steam locomotive practice. It carried an enormous traffic, both in passenger and freight, and between its eastern and western groups of lines lay the Allegheny Mountains, between Altoona and Pittsburgh, where there are long gradients of 1 in 54. The Pennsylvania used locomotives of simple two-cylinder design, of massive strength developed in a continuous tradition, and proved on the famous stationary testing plant at Altoona Works. The fine freight locomotive illustrated in our picture was of a general service type, with coupled wheels as large as 5 ft. 2 in., thus making it suitable for fast goods duties as well as the heaviest haulage on the mountain sections. It was one forming an important link in a chain of development that led to the mighty 'M1a' 4–8–2 of 1930. The 2–8–2 illustrated was introduced in 1918, and had two cylinders 27 in. diameter by 30 in. stroke; the boiler pressure was 205 lb. per sq. in. and the tractive effort 61,465 lb. The boiler was interchangeable with that fitted to the famous 'K4s' Pacifics, which were the mainstay of the express passenger traffic on the Pennsylvania for upwards of twenty years. The 2–8–2 illustrated weighed 140 tons in working order, and 221 tons with its huge tender which carried 9000 gallons of water and $15\frac{1}{2}$ tons of coal.

108 Denver and Rio Grande Western Railroad: A Class 'P-42' 'Pacific' of 1913.

This line was originally a narrow-gauge system running through the heart of the Colorado Rockies; but little by little it was converted to standard gauge, and by the time of the period now under review it boasted a main line 745 miles long from Denver to Salt Lake City. It has been described as 'the scenic line of the world',

from the awe-inspiring nature of some of the mountain country through which it runs. From its picturesque days on the narrow gauge the Rio Grande emerged to become one of the great railways of the U.S.A., and by the year 1910 some exceedingly large freight engines of the Mallet type were at work. They were certainly needed on the gradients experienced in the gorges of the Rocky Mountains. For passenger working the very powerful 'Pacific' illustrated was introduced in 1913. This was no high-speed job, but an engine suited to hard slogging in the mountains. It was a straightforward two-cylinder simple, with a very large boiler and firebox, high-degree superheating, and relatively small coupled wheels. The cylinders were 26 in. diameter by 26 in. stroke; coupled wheels 5 ft. 3 in. diameter; boiler pressure 185 lb. per sq. in., and the high tractive effort of 41,200 lb. The total weight of engine and tender in working order was 192 tons.

109 Great Northern Railway: Gresley Articulated Twin Carriage.

Sir Nigel Gresley will always be remembered for his large main-line steam locomotives; but before he succeeded H. A. Ivatt, as Locomotive Engineer of the Great Northern Railway in 1911, he was Carriage and Wagon Engineer, and in that period he produced, in 1907, a forerunner of a series of remarkably successful mainline coaches. As an experiment to took two ordinary bogie-corridor carriages, and close-coupled them, at the same time mounting the coupled ends over a single bogie. One thus had, virtually, two coaches mounted on three bogies instead of four. This reduced the dead-weight to be hauled by that of one bogie, but what was perhaps more important from the viewpoint of passenger comfort it produced a better ride. When he became Locomotive Engineer of the Great Northern he retained responsibility for carriage and wagon design, and after the First World War he extended the articulated principle to a very interesting quintuple set specially designed for the Leeds service. It combined five coaches in a single articulated unit; but while it gave a beautiful smooth ride and the saving of weight was proportionately greater, as the quintuple unit had only six bogies, the later articulated vehicles introduced on the London and North Eastern Railway, after grouping were triple units mostly consisting of a first-class and third-class dining-car, with kitchen mounted between. The twin unit illustrated was originally used on the London–Edinburgh service.

110 Great Central Railway: Teak-bodied Bogie Corridor Carriage.

When the Manchester, Sheffield, and Lincolnshire Railway built its bitterly contested London extension, and became the Great Central, every conceivable measure was used to advertise the new route. A very new livery was designed for the passenger rolling-stock, with snuff-grey upper panels, and dark chocolate bodies, elaborately lined out. Very smart the new coaches looked—'too smart to be recognized' as a cynical commentator once observed. At any rate, when newer and still more luxurious coaching stock was designed J. G. Robinson, the Chief Mechanical Engineer, reverted to a much plainer finish, with teak match-boarding panels and—strange to say—no lining of any kind. Yet despite this lack of decoration

it is doubtful if there were finer looking main-line coaches anywhere in the world. The proportions were superb; the finish put into the teak was magnificent, and the trains were always kept in the most immaculate condition. Raised brass characters gave the initials G.C.R. a distinguished look, and the destination boards on the roofs were always very comprehensive in their legends. These coaches worked on many cross-country services as well as on the London expresses, and were a splendid advertisement for the Great Central wherever they went.

111 Midland Railway: Elliptical-roofed, Main-line Corridor Carriage.

Until the outbreak of war in 1914, Midland coaching stock had been distinguished by the almost exclusive use of clerestory-roofed carriages, of uniform and beautiful appearance. But several serious accidents, in which collisions led to telescoping and fire, led to a reconsideration of carriage design, and traditional practice was abandoned for a more modern approach. On account of the war construction of the new coaches was delayed, and it was not until 1917 that some of them began to appear in regular main-line workings. As will be seen from our picture they had a more conventional appearance than the older clerestory stock. They were not entirely of steel, but to minimize the effects of a collision the ends and gangways were steel, while the underframes were also of steel. Serious criticism had been made in the case of collisions in 1910 and 1913 of the system of gas lighting used on the Midland Railway. The new coaches were electrically lighted throughout.

Whatever external and structural changes were made, however, the magnificent internal appointments and beautiful paint-work characteristic of the Midland Railway remained. This style of coach became standard in all new construction, until the Midland Railway was absorbed into the L.M.S. system in 1923.

112 Level-Crossings in the U.S.A.: The 'Union' Automatic Flagman.

To British travellers, accustomed to the care and solicitude taken of both railway and road traffic at level-crossings, with completely fenced railways, and the old-style heavily-gated roads, the usual American approach, with unfenced railways, and often little more than an inanimate warning sign at the crossing always seemed a trifle hazardous. In the period of this book with increasing railway speeds, and increasing use of the highways, many ingenious devices were developed to give better warnings at railroad crossings. One of these was produced by one of the largest signalling manufacturers, the Union Switch and Signal Company, of Swissvale, near Pittsburgh. The first of the two illustrations under this reference shows the normal clear aspect, which merely bears the words 'Look, Listen'. When a train is approaching the red disc, carrying the word STOP, was swung out, and continued to swing back and forth, all the time the loud gong on the top of the apparatus was ringing. The swinging disc included a red lamp which was lighted when the disc was in motion so as to give an appropriate indication at night. Despite the provision of such devices, however, many accidents continued to occur, not for lack of warning, but in the majority of cases from motorists endeavouring to beat the train to the crossing!

113 Manual Block Working in the U.S.A.: Double Arm Train Order Signal.

Ordinary manual block working in the U.S.A. was operated on exactly the same principles as in Great Britain. The signals to permit a train to proceed into the next station were lowered mechanically, when telegraphic advice of 'line clear' ahead was received. The blocks were generally the distance between ordinary commercial stations, but sometimes on busy lines, as in Great Britain, intermediate signal boxes—or 'towers' as they are known in the U.S.A.—were installed, in order to shorten the blocks, and at these the arrangement shown in our picture was adopted. The signals were given by what was known as 'train order boards'. These were ordinary three-position semaphore upper-quadrant signals, one for each direction of running, but mounted on the same post, which in itself was just in front of the station building or 'tower'. A curious arrangement was that the operating levers for the two signals were on different floors, involving the 'towerman' in a certain amount of running up and down stairs. There was no inter-locking, or any other safety link-up with adjoining 'towers'.

114 Ouhd and Rohilkund Railway (India): Signalling at Cawnpore Bridge over the River Ganges.

This one-time independent railway, running between Lucknow and Cawnpore, crossed the River Ganges on the outskirts of Cawnpore by a single-line railway bridge. Accommodation had to be provided for both the Indian broad-gauge, of 5 ft. 6 in., and also metre-gauge trains, and the railway passed through picturesque blockhouses on each side of the river. On one side there was situated Cawnpore Bridge Station, with five running lines—two broad-gauge and three metre-gauge, and on the other side of the river there were the separate broad- and narrow-gauge lines, both single-tracked. Our picture shows the blockhouse looking towards Cawnpore Bridge Station, surmounted by five semaphore signals, one for each of the lines in the station area. The actual signalling was rendered more complicated by the existence of a road level-crossing immediately beyond the blockhouse, and special precautions had to be taken to ensure that road traffic was stopped, and the gates closed. In India, in urban areas the level-crossings were frequently protected by gates as in British practice.

115 Level Crossing Gate: British Practice.

Regulations for railway working in Great Britain demand that the line shall be fully fenced throughout, using walling, open fencing, or hedging, so as to minimize the risk of animals, or trespassers from straying on the line. Where roads of any kind cross the railway gates have to be provided, though nowadays many of these are being replaced by lifting barriers. Gate operation is generally of one of three kinds. In urban areas, or where main roads cross railways, the gates are operated from near-by signal-boxes and the gate gear is interlocked with the signal and point levers, thus ensuring that the signals cannot be lowered until the gates are set against road traffic and duly locked in that position. In less busy locations what are termed 'gate boxes' are installed. The gates are opened, or closed by pushing them round by hand; but the 'gate box' is in communication with the adjacent signal-boxes, and the gates are not opened to road traffic unless it is ascertained that no train is expected. Such crossings are protected by signals, and these cannot be lowered unless the gates are set across the roadway and locked in that position. The third category is the so-called 'occupation crossing', usually installed for the convenience of farmers, or other members of the rural community. These are not usually level-crossing gates in the ordinary sense but small gates in the fences, or walls at the side of the line. There is no interlocking and persons crossing the line do so at their own risk.

116 Level Crossing Wicket Gates: British Practice.

Where there is considerable pedestrian traffic over a level crossing it is customary to provide small side, or wicket gates on the footpath beside a main road. These gates are usually spring-controlled, being held in the position, closing the footpath against railway traffic, but capable of being pushed open by hand. This saves the expense of having special operating gear for the wicket gates; but when the main gates are closed across the roadway to permit the passage of a train, the wicket gates are locked at the same time as the main gates are locked.

117 Great Western Railway: 2-6-0 Fast Mixed Traffic Locomotive.

It is appropriate to begin reference to the Mogul type in Great Britain with G. J. Churchward's very successful '43XX' class. Although constituting an entirely new design from Swindon Works it was in effect a synthesis of standard parts using cylinders, motion, coupled wheels and boiler that were all interchangeable with those of certain existing standard locomotives. It was designed to provide enhanced power for fast goods, intermediate passenger and excursion traffic, and to be capable of use over a high proportion of the total mileage of the company. The design proved an outstanding success, and eventually several hundreds of them were at work. At one time they were responsible for practically the entire main-line work in Cornwall, both passenger and goods, while in express passenger service they had been recorded at speeds in excess of 75 m.p.h. The cylinders were $18\frac{1}{2}$ in. diameter by 30 in. stroke, with piston valves operated by the Stephenson link motion inside; the coupled-wheel diameter was 5 ft. 8 in., and the boiler pressure 200 lb. per sq. in. The total weight of the engine only in working order was 62 tons. The boiler was of the taper-barrelled type very carefully developed at Swindon with Belpaire firebox also of a highly specialized and successful design. As originally built, and as illustrated, these engines were finished in the full, ornate, passenger livery.

118 **Caledonian Railway:** The McIntosh 2–6–0 Express Goods Locomotive.

Great operating success, and substantial economies in coal consumption, had been achieved by the application of superheating to the express passenger 4–4–0s of the Caledonian Railway and, requiring a more powerful engine for the sharply-timed residential trains between Glasgow and the Clyde Coast, McIntosh built a mixed traffic 0–6–0 with 5 ft. wheels, that could accelerate very rapidly. The overhanging weight at the front end was considerable,

and when the success of the Clyde Coast 0–6–0s suggested using the same type for the faster main-line goods trains the 2–6–0 wheel arrangement was adopted to get a smoother riding engine. They were the first locomotives of the 2–6–0 type to be built for a Scottish railway, and the five engines of the class, all built at the St Rollox Works of the Caledonian Railway in 1912, did good work on the main line between Glasgow and Carlisle for upwards of twenty years. Their 0–6–0 predecessors, on the Clyde Coast residential trains, were painted in the famous Caledonian blue livery; but the 2–6–0s as shown in our picture were finished in what was termed 'goods black'. Their cylinders were $19\frac{1}{2}$ in. diameter by 26 in. stroke; coupled wheels 5 ft. 0 in. diameter; boiler pressure 160 lb. per sq. in., and tractive effort 22,409 lb.

119 **London Brighton and South Coast Railway:** 2–6–0 Fast Goods Locomotive.

The Brighton railway followed the prevailing fashion of the years just preceding the First World War, by introducing the 2–6–0 type for fast mixed traffic working. The service that needed particular attention was the so-called 'Grande Vitesse' continental goods business via Newhaven and Dieppe. The first L.B. & S.C.R. 2–6–0s were built in 1913 and further engines of the class were added to cope with the extra traffic of wartime. Then, in 1920, their designer, Colonel L. B. Billinton, introduced certain important modifications into the design in some further engines of the class. Some of the exhaust steam was used to heat the feed water to the boiler, and thus saved fuel by delivering the water into the boiler hotter than it would otherwise have been. But the most conspicuous change was the addition of what appears to be a second dome on the boiler. This is actually the apparatus for feeding the water into the boiler at the very top, instead of through the more conventional clack valves on the side. 'Top-feed', as it was generally known, had been standardized by that time on the Great Western, but the distinction in the Brighton case was the height of the casing. These engines had two cylinders 21 in. diameter by 26 in. stroke; 5 ft. 6 in. diameter coupled wheels, and carried a boiler pressure of 170 lb. per sq. in.

120 **Great Northern Railway:** The '1000' Class Three-cylinder 2–6–0.

At the end of the First World War there was great speculation in the British locomotive world as to the nature of a large new engine known to be under construction at the Doncaster works of the Great Northern Railway. Mr Gresley, as he then was, had already built a fleet of two-cylinder 2–6–0s; he had greatly improved the famous Ivatt 'Atlantics', and it was rumoured that he was bringing out a large 2–6–2 express locomotive. But when the new engine did appear it turned out to be a greatly enlarged version of the 2–6–0, with three cylinders, a boiler of the largest diameter yet seen on any British locomotive, and an ingenious arrangement of valve gear in which only two sets of gear were needed for actuating the valves of all three cylinders. These engines, of which ten were built in 1920, proved a great success. Although designated 'mixed traffic' they proved capable of speeds of 75 m.p.h., and could work express passenger trains of great weight in emergency. The original ten locomotives were finished in the

beautiful passenger engine livery of the Great Northern Railway, but after the grouping of the railways in 1923 they were adopted as an L.N.E.R. standard and classified 'K3'. No fewer than 183 more of them were built for service all over the system, and the class was then painted black with red lining.

121 **London and North Western Railway:** Local Mineral Train Brake Van.

The vast amount of short-distance local goods and mineral traffic on the British railways was a particular feature of this age of railway supremacy. Our picture shows a standard 20-ton L.N.W.R. brake van for use on loose-coupled goods trains on which the only brake power was that which could be exerted by the engine, and the hand-applied brake of the guard's van. If one had to descend a steep gradient on which there was a danger of the weight of the wagons overpowering this modest brake power, then a stop had to be made at the top of the gradient, and a certain number of wagons had their individual hand brakes pinned down. In many industrial areas traffic was regular enough for specific brake vans and engines to be allocated to them, and our picture shows a typical example: 'Clock Face & Springs Branch'. Clock Face is the name of a large colliery in the Wigan area of Lancashire, and Springs Branch is the main-line junction about a mile south of Wigan where traffic from the numerous collieries in the district was brought together for marshalling into full-length trains for the long main-line hauls. As its naming implies the Clock Face van was used exclusively for coal from the one colliery.

122 **Great Central Railway:** 30-ton All-steel Bogie Coal Wagon.

The years of railway pre-eminence were times of anxiety and frustration to many British railway operators, who were saddled with the layouts and equipment designed and built up over seventy or eighty years, entirely around the conventional four-wheeled vehicles, with loose chain couplings and no continuous brakes. The advantages of working larger wagons were obvious enough where large consignments of homogenous material, such as coal, ore, or bricks were involved; but there would be no advantage of running large wagons if they were likely to be filled with an assortment of small packages, or articles of all shapes and sizes. Coal was an ideal traffic for bulk consignment, if only the larger wagons could be accommodated at the loading and discharge points. With locomotive fuel the railways did have at least one end of the transit under their own control, and the Great Central 30-ton wagon illustrated indicates that it had been found economic to load into these large wagons at certain selected pits, and so design the locomotive running sheds to accommodate their receipt. On the London Extension of the railway, opened in 1899, they certainly had the opportunity to build in a more modern way, and the wagon illustrated is a fine example of bulk-transportation.

123 **Great Western Railway:** 30-ton Bogie covered Van.

The large bogie covered van illustrated is another interesting example of the trend towards larger vehicles that was manifest in the early years of the period covered by this book. Great importance was justifiably attached to the freight traffic arriving from overseas at the Bristol and Avonmouth Docks, and its rapid transit to London. These large vans were built specially for the fast night goods trains on which the majority, if not all of the vehicles were fitted with the vacuum-continuous automatic brake. With this provision these trains could be run up to speeds of about 55 m.p.h. on favourable stretches of track. The high priority given to the working of the eastbound fast goods from Bristol was shown by the use, for several years, of the huge 'Pacific' engine *The Great Bear* on this nightly run. It would work down from Paddington to Bristol on the evening Plymouth dining-car express, and then return to London during the night with the very heavy express goods. The Great Western Railway developed the design of express goods vehicles for special consignments, such as meat, and particularly bananas from the West Indies. The vehicle illustrated was, however, for general purpose traffic.

124 **London and North Western Railway:** Cattle Box for Working on Passenger Trains.

This was a period when great attention was given to the requirements of individual customers where special attention was demanded. Families could engage private saloon carriages for themselves and their servants to be conveyed from anywhere to anywhere. It was the same with valuable animals, such as bloodstock and valuable cattle. Our picture shows a 'cattle box' designed for conveyance in express passenger trains, and including a separate compartment for the herdsman and any assistants. The normal colour of the L.N.W.R. freight vehicles, both open and covered was dark grey; but these vehicles designed for inclusion in express passenger trains were painted in the dark purple brown of the passenger stock. They were of course fitted with continuous brakes; but that was not all. While the North Western used the vacuum brake, the Caledonian used the Westinghouse, so that to render these cattle boxes suitable for Anglo-Scottish working they were dual-fitted, with both brakes, like the West Coast Joint passenger stock.

125 London and North Western Railway: The 'George the Fifth' Class 4-4-0 Express Passenger Locomotive.

This remarkable English design of 1910 had as its structural foundation the 'Precursor', 4-4-0 of 1904—another of the famous products of Crewe Works. The chassis was identical, so was the size of the boiler barrel and the firebox; but there the similarity ended. The 'George the Fifth' had a Schmidt superheater, providing a high degree of superheat in the steam, and an extensive change from the 'Precursor' in its design of cylinders, valves, and valve gear. The result was a locomotive that for its size was capable of an almost phenomenal output of power. The general standard of express train timings on the L.N.W.R. was an average speed of about 55 m.p.h., start to stop, and the 'George the Fifth' class engines, of which there were originally ninety, maintained these schedules easily with trains of 400 tons. Indeed, in cases of delay, when time had to be made up, the average speeds were stepped up to 60 m.p.h. or even more. One of these engines, built in 1911, and named *Coronation*, was the five-thousandth locomotive to be built at Crewe Works. It was unfortunate that

these otherwise brilliantly successful engines were built on the same chassis as the less powerful 'Precursors' and the great power they developed caused troubles with the frames. With increasing age they became heavy on maintenance costs, and had to be relegated to lighter duties. But in their prime, during the years 1910–16, they were incomparable.

126 Great Northern Railway: The '56' Class 4-4-0 Express Passenger Locomotive.

Among the top British 4-4-0s of the period of this book, the ten locomotives of the Great Northern '56' class are probably the least known. Unlike most British railways the Great Northern made little use of the 4-4-0 for first-class express service. Transition came, with little intermission, from the ever-famous Stirling 'singles' of the nineteenth century to the Ivatt 'Atlantics', and the various designs of 4-4-0 introduced during the Ivatt régime, were to some extent a family of 'step-children'. Yet in the last of them, the '56' class which were superheated, the Great Northern had an excellent medium-powered engine. They worked mostly north of Grantham, and there are several recorded occasions of them doing splendid work with the heavy Scottish expresses when called upon to deputise for an 'Atlantic' and run a 400-ton train from Grantham to York non-stop. After the grouping of the railways in 1923, when the Scottish area of the L.N.E.R. was short of engine power all ten of them were sent north. Instead of 56 to 65 they became 3056 to 3065, and being no more than second-line units were painted black. Although the arrangement of the various controls on their footplates were so different from what the Scottish enginemen had been used to, they did much useful work, some of it in assisting larger engines on the very heavy East Coast expresses between Edinburgh and Dundee.

127 Midland Railway: The '999' Class 4-4-0 Express Passenger Locomotive.

At the turn of the century, the Midland Railway had stepped into the very fore-front of British locomotive practice by the production at Derby Works of the very celebrated three-cylinder Smith-Johnson compounds. Although a great deal of experimenting with compound locomotives had taken place in Great Britain these Midland compounds, of which five were built for trial purposes, were the first that could be called thorough-ly successful. But they were complicated engines to manage, and Johnson's suc-cessor, R. M. Deeley, brought out a modi-fied version, with much simplified controls for the drivers. Although the Deeley compounds lacked the finer points that a skilful engineman could get out of the Johnson originals they were adequate for the traffic of the day, and a total of forty were built. At the same time Deeley was not entirely convinced of the advantages of compounding for the running conditions then prevailing on the Midland Railway and in 1907 he built ten locomotives of comparable power to the compounds, but as two-cylinder simples. Our picture shows one of these engines as modernized by the addition of a superheater. They worked over the heavily graded line between Leeds and Carlisle, which reached an altitude of 1151 ft. above sea-level at Aisgill summit. The ten engines of the class did good work over this line for nearly twenty years, though in com-parative tests they were shown to have neither the hauling power nor the economy of the Midland compounds when the latter were superheated.

128 Glasgow and South Western Railway: Four-cylinder 4-4-0 Express Locomotive *Lord Glenarthur*.

As a locomotive designer, Robert H. Whitelegg was a very frustrated man. He had no sooner succeeded his father as Locomotive Superintendent of the Lon-don, Tilbury, and Southend Railway, when that line was taken over by the Midland. The story of his big 4-6-4 tank engine may be found under reference 149; and then after he had succeeded Peter Drummond on the Glasgow and South Western, there came the grouping and that line became part of the L.M.S. system. Just before the merger, however, White-legg produced what was virtually a new express passenger design by an extensive rebuilding of Britain's first four-cylinder simple locomotive, a 4-4-0 built at Kilmarnock by James Manson, in 1897. The old chassis and wheels were used, but everything else was new, and *Lord Glenarthur* could well have been the prototype for a new and successful class of express passenger engines. As it was, in fact, the locomotive remained the only one of its kind, albeit a most handsome and powerful unit. All four cylinders drove on to the leading pair of coupled wheels, and simplification of the machinery between the frames was achieved by what is termed 'cross-porting', making it possible for one piston valve to control the steam of both cylinders on one side of the engine. Only two sets of valve gear were required. As originally built the strokes of the inside and outside cylinders differed: 24 in.

outside and 26 in. inside. This feature was retained, with all four cylinders having a diameter of 14 in. The coupled wheels were 6 ft. $9\frac{1}{2}$ in. diameter; the boiler pressure was 180 lb. per sq. in., and the tractive effort was 18,390 lb.

129 Bern–Lötschberg–Simplon Railway: The Lötschberg Tunnel, North Façade.

In the summer of 1913 a great new trunk route through the Alps was completed by the opening of the celebrated B.L.S. line between Spiez, on the Lake of Thun, and Brig, at the Swiss end of the Simplon Tunnel. The Lötschberg line, electrically operated from the outset, is one of the most dramatic pieces of railway engineering in Europe, carried among the giant mountain ranges of the Bernese Oberland. The approaches to the great tunnel itself are on continuously severe gradients, on a single-tracked line carried mainly on precipitous mountain sides, and today it is subject to a speed-limit of 47 m.p.h. But except for a slight detour near the centre the tunnel is relatively straight, and double-tracked, and with the great international express trains passing north and south through this part of Switzerland the highest speeds are usually attained in the middle of the tunnel. It is just over nine miles long and as the dates on the façade in our picture indicate it took some six years to build, 1906 to 1912. The picture is interesting as showing the French spelling of the name *Loetschberg*. This district is predominantly German-speaking, until the southern end of the B.L.S. line, where the proximity of the Italian frontier gives rise to a marked change in dialect, which is not always understood by those who live in central Switzerland.

130 Great Western Railway: Box Tunnel, Eastern Portal.

It is perhaps no exaggeration to suggest that this is one of the most famous of British railway tunnels. It is certainly one of the earliest, and formed part of the original main line of the Great Western Railway and was opened in 1841. The great I. K. Brunel engineered a route of remarkably even gradient for that line, except in effecting the traverse from the high ground at the head of the Vale of the White Horse, beyond Swindon, to the entry to the lower Avon valley at Bathampton. Here he could not avoid some sharp gradients, and in cutting through the limestone ridge west of Corsham he used a gradient of 1 in 100 for nearly two miles. Whether he did so intentionally or otherwise we do not know, but the fact remains that the line and tunnel are so located that the rising sun shines through the tunnel from end to end on one day in the year, in April, and that so near to the engineer's own birthday as to suggest he contrived it deliberately. The western end of the tunnel, in the pleasant village of Box, has a colossal classical façade; but the eastern end shown in our picture is of interest as showing not only the railway tunnel, but on the left the entrance to some underground limestone quarries deep in the *massif* of Box Hill. In later years the comparative safety of the huge caverns excavated was utilized for the production of war material in the Second World War. The Box Tunnel itself is 1·8 miles long.

131 Chester and Holyhead Railway: Bangor Tunnel, Western Portal.

In the title I have used the original name of this celebrated line engineered by

Robert Stephenson. At an early stage in British railway history there was keen controversy over the route to be adopted for conveyance of the Irish Mail, between London and Dublin. I. K. Brunel recommended an extension of the broad-gauge Great Western line from Oxford westwards through the mountains of central Wales to an entirely new packet station on the Lledr peninsula, while Stephenson proposed an extension of existing standard gauge lines from Chester along the North Wales coast through Conway and Bangor, and thence across the Isle of Anglesey. Stephenson's proposals were accepted, and in decorating the numerous major engineering works on the route he introduced magnificent portals to the tunnels and decorating work at the principal stations. The line later became one of the trunk routes of the London and North Western Railway. The western end of the Bangor Tunnel, which can be clearly seen from the station platforms, includes an Egyptian style of architecture, somewhat obscured by the bridge of signals, mounted as low as possible to facilitate sighting by the drivers of trains approaching through the tunnel. After more than a hundred years of steam traction, the tunnel façade has become generally blackened by smoke, and its fine features are less clearly discernible from the station platform.

132 **London and North Western Railway:** Morley Tunnel, the Western Portal, between Leeds and Dewsbury.

The various railway connections between the large towns of the West Riding of Yorkshire and those clustered around Manchester, involve heavy gradients and difficult engineering works. The main east–west route of the London and North Western Railway was typical in this respect, climbing steeply out of Airedale, descending to the Calder Valley, and then rising again more prolongedly through Huddersfield to a summit level in tunnel beneath some of the highest ridges of this part of the Pennines. At both these summit points there are long tunnels—Standedge, indeed, is one of the longest in Great Britain. Our picture shows the western portal of the other one, Morley, which is 1·9 miles long. This has been chosen for illustration because of its highly distinctive architectural style. While other façades portrayed classic, or other neo-classic, forms a very striking effect was achieved at Morley west end by extending the basic elliptical arch of the tunnel bore itself out into the open, and finishing it with massive stone mouldings. One is always tempted to wonder why such individual styles were adopted, especially so at Morley; for whereas the eastern end was close to the platform ends at Morley station, the striking western end illustrated was set in bleak moorland country where the only persons in a position to appreciate it would be the surface men, and the drivers and firemen of trains about to enter. Nowadays, of course, passengers in diesel railcars can see it.

133 **Servian State Railways:** 0–10–0 Two-cylinder Compound Freight Engine.

The success of the Gölsdorf compound locomotives in Austria had a considerable influence elsewhere, and in Servia, as Serbia was commonly known before the First World War, the existence of very heavy gradients and the absence of any need for very fast running, led to the introduction of many small-wheel multi- coupled locomotives. In 1909 the Servian State Railways purchased some 0–10–0 tender locomotives from the celebrated German firm of A. Borsig, of Berlin, and as will be seen from our picture they were about the most uncontinental looking locomotives one could possibly imagine. With their handsomely shaped chimneys, 'clean' lines, and almost complete absence of 'gadgets' hung on outside they would have made a distinguished addition to the stock of the English Great Central Railway! A curious design feature was the very long piston rod, with the slide bars arranged opposite to the second pair of coupled wheels. This was done to avoid an excessive length of connecting-rod, through the drive being made on to the fourth pair of coupled wheels. The two cylinders had diameters of $22\frac{1}{16}$ in. high pressure and $33\frac{1}{2}$ in. low pressure, both with a stroke of $24\frac{7}{8}$ in. The coupled-wheel diameter was 4 ft. $3\frac{3}{4}$ in., and the boiler pressure 200 lb. per sq. in. From this it will be appreciated that these were not only very handsome, but also very powerful locomotives.

134 Egyptian State Railways: 4–6–0 Express Passenger Locomotive.

In the years 1912–13 the Egyptian State Railways was conducting a series of most interesting experiments with different types of locomotives, on its straight and generally level main line of 130 miles between Cairo and Alexandria, and it can be said that it was these trials that largely inspired the design of the 'Atlantic' engine (ref. 87). The trials involved the older standard 4–4–0 locomotives, some of the De Glehn compound 'Atlantics' which were identical with those of the Northern Railway of France, and the 4–6–0 type of express locomotive illustrated in our picture. The task set was the haulage of a

train of 330 tons over that 130 miles at an average speed of 43 m.p.h. This would not be a difficult task in calm weather, but it is another matter altogether when the prevailing wind is blowing strongly across this exposed track. The 4–6–0 illustrated proved capable enough, but a heavy coal-burner, and it was the performance of one of the older 4–4–0s fitted with a Schmidt superheater that surpassed all, and pointed clearly the way towards future development. The 4–6–0s had cylinders 19 in. diameter by 26 in. stroke; coupled wheels 6 ft. 3 in. diameter, and a boiler pressure of 180 lb. per sq. in.

135 Great Southern and Western Railway: 4–6–0 Heavy Goods and Mixed Traffic Engines.

The first years of the present century were times of prosperity and expansion in Ireland, and the locomotive department of the G.S. & W.R. at Inchicore, Dublin, under the superintendence of R. A. Coey, was very active. At that same time R. E. L. Maunsell, who was later to become famous as Chief Mechanical Engineer of the Southern Railway in England, was Works Manager at Inchicore. At the end of 1905 the first locomotive of the 4–6–0 type to run on one of the Irish main-line railways was completed. The six engines of this class were designed for heavy main-line goods traffic much of which originated from the calling of transatlantic liners at Queenstown (now Cobh). The Inchicore Works modelled much of its practice upon that of Crewe, including the style of paintings of its locomotives. Inside cylinders were the rule, and a pleasing neatness of outline characterized all designs, passenger and goods alike. The two cylinders were $19\frac{1}{4}$ in. diameter by 26 in. stroke; coupled-wheel diameter was 5 ft. $1\frac{3}{4}$ in., and the boiler pressure 160 lb. per sq. in. They were not superheated. The total weight of engine and tender in working order was 92 tons.

136 San Paulo Railway Brazil: 2–8–0 Freight Locomotives.

The San Paulo Railway was one of the many British-owned railway systems in South America, and it traversed a difficult mountain country on its 86-mile long main line from the port of Santos to San Paulo City and Jundiahy, where it made an end-on junction with the Paulista Railway. The gauge is not the South American broad-gauge standard of 5 ft. 6 in. but 5 ft. 3 in. This railway was taken over by the Federal Government of Brazil in 1946, and renamed the Estrada de Ferro Santos a Jundiai. As existing prior to the First World War the main line was double-tracked throughout, but included some gradients of 1 in 40. It was nevertheless a finely engineered line, and speeds up to 62 m.p.h. were permitted. The engine illustrated was one of a series of ten built in 1909 by the North British Locomotive Company at their Atlas Works, Springburn, Glasgow. They were powerful engines, of a simple yet very robust design well suited to the hard work demanded. The cylinders were $21\frac{1}{2}$ in. diameter by 26 in. stroke; coupled wheels were 4 ft. 6 in. diameter, and the boiler pressure was 200 lb. per sq. in. The boiler was a large one, fitted with Schmidt superheater, and the cylinders were fed through piston valves of the Schmidt patent type as extensively used in England on the London and North Western Railway.

137 North Eastern Railway: First-class Dining car.

The North Eastern Railway, as the largest and wealthiest partner in the group of companies operating the East Coast route from London to Scotland, contributed some notable coaching stock to the jointly operated services. But joint services over the North Eastern Railway were not confined to Anglo-Scottish traffic. There was an important and very popular cross-country service between Newcastle and Liverpool, worked jointly with the Lancashire and Yorkshire Railway for which each company provided a luxurious corridor, dining-car train that worked on each service on alternate days. These beautiful set-trains each consisted of seven carriages, as follows: a brake van; two third-class carriages; third-class saloon, used as required as a dining-car; a combined third-class diner and kitchen car; first-class dining-car; a corridor brake van; and first-class car. The carriages were all arranged to have entrances only at the end vestibules, and these were of reduced width to keep the handles within the loading gauge limit. The coach bodies were built out to the maximum to provide the greatest amount of space inside for passenger comfort. With the exception of the combined kitchen and third-class dining-car, which was a twelve-wheeler, the remaining coaches in the train were all eight-wheelers. Our picture shows the first-class dining-car, the general style of which was followed in all the coaches of this fine train.

138 North Eastern Railway: First-class Dining car (Interior).

The interior style of the first-class dining-car in these 'set' trains is worthy of special notice as it embodies some of the finest practice of the day, in British railway carriage construction. Two of these 'set' trains were built, and the style of decoration in the dining-room cars differed. One was finished throughout in dark walnut, having quartered panels of Pollard walnut of fine figure, inlaid with bands of pine edged with ebony and boxwood. The woodwork of the other car was in mahogany. The standard colour of upholstery in first-class accommodation on the North Eastern Railway was then in dark blue Melton cloth, and to set this off, in relation to the colours of the fine woodwork in the cars, curtains and trimmings of a russet tint were used, while brown and orange were included in the pattern of the carpets. The pleasing scheme of decoration, which will be apparent from our picture, was devised and executed entirely by the York carriage works of the North Eastern Railway. It should be added that while one of these trains worked on the Liverpool–Newcastle service, the second was used on the summer service operated jointly with the Great Northern Railway between London, Scarborough, and Whitby. Similar trains were introduced later on to the Anglo-Scottish service between Leeds, Edinburgh, and Glasgow.

139 London Brighton and South Coast Railway: First-class Pullman car.

The pioneer work of the American carriage designer George M. Pullman, was not at first directed to the production of luxury vehicles. He introduced large and easy-riding cars for running over the lightly laid tracks of the U.S.A., and they took various forms, including both day and night saloons. In England they were first introduced on the Midland Railway in 1876, but it was undoubtedly on the London, Brighton, and South Coast Railway that they achieved their greatest popularity in the period now under review, and it was this that induced the enterprising management to put on the first daily all-Pullman train in Great Britain, from November 1908 onwards. Four times a day it covered the 51 miles between Victoria and Brighton in the even hour, and its coaches were the height of luxury. The train was christened *The Southern Belle*, and for the first thirteen years of its existence it was first-class only. The maximum load was limited to seven of the massive cars illustrated and their beautiful décor blended perfectly with the chocolate brown locomotives, the painting style—though not on an express engine—can be seen from reference 119. All the first-class cars were named; but when third-class Pullmans were put on, in 1921, they bore only numbers, though having the same splendid external finish.

140 London Brighton and South Coast Railway: Parlour Saloon (Interior).

In general this railway did not use corridor carriages on its main-line trains, and generally the only way in which passengers could obtain a little extra luxury or the facility of refreshments *en route* was to travel in the Pullman cars attached to many of the principal expresses. But the 'City Limited', often referred to as the Stockbrokers' Special was in a class by itself. It left Brighton at 8.45 a.m. and ran non-stop to London Bridge in the even hour. In the evening it left at 5 p.m. and again made a non-stop run to Brighton. In 1907 some very fine vestibuled non-Pullman carriages were built specially for this train, for the exclusive use of first-class passengers the majority of whom would be season-ticket holders and daily travellers. The corridor coaches were of the conventional type, containing six compartments, each seating six passengers; but there were in addition parlour saloons, the interior of one of which is shown in our picture. The seating included a number of movable wicker chairs and some fixed seats. The regular clientele of these fine trains was much the same as those of the 'club' trains run from Manchester to various seaside destinations. Passengers would have their regular parties of business friends, and the casual traveller might well find some difficulty in finding a seat!

141 Bulgarian State Railways: 2–8–0 Four-cylinder Compound Freight Engine.

In the years before the outbreak of the First World War the State Railways of Bulgaria attracted special attention in the British railway press through the personal interest in their activities shown by their King. He not only rode on locomotives at intervals, but was a fully competent engineman, and used to drive the Royal Train himself. The State Railway system from its very inception presented problems in motive power, due to the very severe gradients. The system is remarkable in never having had any four-coupled locomotives, even in its earliest days. The 2–8–0 locomotive shown in our picture was one of a class designed for heavy freight working, and built in Germany by the Hannoversche Machinenbau Actien Gesellschaft in 1911. The cylinder diameters were $14\frac{3}{4}$ in. high pressure, $23\frac{5}{8}$ in. low pressure, both having a stroke of $25\frac{5}{8}$ in. All four cylinders drove on to the second pair of coupled wheels. The

coupled wheels had a diameter of 4 ft. 1 in., and the boiler pressure was 213 lb. per sq. in. The spark-arrester device on the chimney will be specially noted. The leading pair of coupled wheels are incorporated with the small carrying wheels in a swivelling 'Helmholtz' truck, as used on the Austrian 2–6–4 express engines (ref. 22). In consequence the rigid wheelbase was only 12 ft. making the engine readily adaptable to sharp curvature in the line. In later batches of these engines larger coupled wheels were used, and the type became a general utility standard in Bulgaria.

142 Chilean State Railways: 4–6–0 Express Passenger Locomotive of 1913.

The republic of Chile is one of the most unusual geographical entities in the world. In length the country measures nearly 3000 miles, and yet the average width is less than 100 miles. The whole country is mountainous, and its eastern frontier lies along the summits of the rugged chain of the Andes. The railway system reflects the geography of the country, and includes primarily one long main line extending from Santiago to Puerto Montt. Part of the system, between Valparaiso and Santiago was chosen early for electrification, and contracts for this were let in 1921; but during the period of this book steam haulage prevailed, and the total stock of around 600 locomotives included British, German, and American types in considerable variety. The locomotive chosen for illustration is clearly one designed under British influence, though it was actually one of a batch supplied from the U.S.A., by Baldwins, in 1913. It is a straightforward two-cylinder simple, with Walschaerts valve gear. The cylinders were 20 in. diameter by 26 in. stroke; coupled-wheel diameter was 5 ft. 6 in., and boiler pressure 175 lb. per sq. in. The total weight of engine only in working order was 62 tons. The typically British boiler mountings are conspicuous, and it bears quite a marked resemblance to some contemporary Indian locomotives, designed and built in Great Britain.

143 Gotthard Railway: 2–8–0 Four-cylinder Compound Freight Locomotive.

It is perhaps no exaggeration to say that the grandly-picturesque line leading up from the Lake of Lucerne to the great Gotthard Tunnel, and then down into the Italian-speaking Swiss canton of Ticino is the hardest ever to be worked by steam on the continent of Europe. From Erstfeld there is a continuous ascent of 1 in 38–39 for *eighteen miles* to the tunnel entrance at Göschenen, and in that distance the line passes through twenty-one shorter tunnels, crosses sixteen bridges of more than 16 ft. span, and negotiates several spiral locations to keep the gradient at an even figure. There is an equally severe descent from the southern end of the Gotthard Tunnel at Airolo. The Gotthard Railway was originally an independent concern, and during the period of this book most of its locomotives were purchased from the Munich firm of J.A. Maffei, specialists in compound engines. The railway used 4–6–0s for passenger, and for freight the interesting 2–8–0 type illustrated in our picture were used. The cylinder diameters were $15\frac{1}{2}$ in. high pressure (inside the frames) and 25 in. low pressure, with a common stroke of $25\frac{1}{8}$ in. The coupled-wheel diameter was 4 ft. $5\frac{1}{4}$ in., and the boiler pressure 220 lb. per sq. in. Both 4–6–0 and 2–8–0 types introduced in 1908

had the Maffei type of steam drier, rather than superheaters. The valve gear was the Heusinger design, very similar in its steam distribution and layout to the Walschaerts.

144 Bavarian State Railways: Mallet Compound Articulated 0–8–8–0 Tank Engine.

Two through routes of the Bavarian State Railways over which important passenger train services were operated included some severe mountain sections with gradients of 1 in 40; these were the Würzburg–Aschaffenburg and the Bamberg–Hallé lines. A very powerful type of locomotive was required for banking, and the Mallet articulated type was chosen. It is important to recall that although the Mallet type of articulation is normally associated with the U.S.A. it originated in Europe, and the very first large Mallet was built by Maffei of Munich for the Gotthard Railway. The huge 0–8–8–0 illustrated was also built by Maffei in 1913, and it was required to assist passenger trains so as to ensure a speed of $20\frac{1}{2}$ m.p.h. on the 1 in 40 gradients. As usual in compound Mallets the high-pressure cylinders drive the rear group of wheels and the low-pressure the forward group. The coupled-wheel diameter was 4 ft. 0 in. The controls admit live steam to be admitted direct to the low-pressure cylinders in certain conditions. The high-pressure cylinders were $20\frac{1}{2}$ in. diameter, and the low pressure $31\frac{1}{2}$ in., both having a stroke of $25\frac{3}{16}$ in. The boiler pressure was 212 lb. per sq. in., and the total weight of the locomotive in working order was $122\frac{1}{2}$ tons. The tractive effort was 42,000 lb. As such, these remarkable machines were the heaviest and most powerful tank engines in Europe.

145 **Central Railway of Brazil:** 0-6-6-0 Mallet Articulated Compound Freight Engine.

The Mallet system of articulation was used for heavy freight and bank engine duties in every continent in the world. It is natural that it was never tried in Great Britain, where the need to provide exceptional power for freight trains did not arise (*see* ref. 7). The Mallet was built by all three of the great American manufacturers, and an interesting example of what could be termed a medium- powered engine, for a Mallet, is afforded by this 0-6-6-0 built for Brazil by the American Locomotive Co. (familiarly known as ALCO). This Brazilian engine, without any guiding wheels, front or rear, was essentially a slow-speed job, of characteristic American appearance. It had the usual Mallet arrangement of cylinders, the high pressure being beneath the centre of the boiler, and the low 'out front'. The cylinder diameters were $17\frac{1}{2}$ in. high pressure, with piston valves, 28 in. low pressure, with slide valves. The stroke of both was 26 in. The coupled-wheel diameter was 4 ft. 2 in. and the boiler pressure 200 lb. per sq. in. Arrangements were included so that the locomotive could be worked for short periods as a simple, with the high tractive effort of 50,900 lb. When working normally as a compound the tractive effort was 42,400 lb. The weight of engine alone in working order was 92 tons. This engine was, of course, working on the 5 ft. 3 in. and not the metre-gauge section of the railway.

146 **Erie Railroad:** Triple Articulated Mallet Compound.

The constant drive to obtain greater power per unit of weight on the locomotives of

the U.S.A. led to some remarkable designs, of which the Santa Fé freighter with *flexible* boiler, has already been noted (ref. 50). In this diverse collection of Mallet articulated locomotives the 'triple' Erie 2–8–8–8–2 was outstanding. One of these extraordinary machines was built by Baldwins in 1914 for trial, and this proving satisfactory two further engines to the same design were supplied in 1916. As will be seen from our picture there were *three* engine units, and the cylinders of these were all of the same size, namely 36 in. diameter by 32 in. stroke. But the locomotive was nevertheless a compound. Only the cylinders driving the middle group of wheels took live steam from the boiler, at a pressure of 210 lb. per sq. in. One high-pressure cylinder exhausted into the two front cylinders and the other into the two rear cylinders. The tractive effort was 160,000 lb., and the total weight of the combined engine and steam-driven tender unit, no less than 380 tons. These locomotives were used solely on banking duties on the Susquehanna Hill, developing a very high tractive effort at low speed. Despite their undoubted success on this duty for which they were specially designed they remained the only ones of the type ever built.

147 **Chicago, Burlington, and Quincy Railroad:** A 2–6–6–2 Mallet Compound of 1909.

The 'Burlington Road', as it is generally known today, has become celebrated as one of the earlier American railways to exploit the possibilities of high-speed streamlined service with diesel-electric locomotives, and the 'Burlington Zephyr' was one of the most distinctive of such early high-speed trains. But the railway has always been far more than a passenger 'speedway', and its freight traffic was such as to demand loco-motives of the highest tractive effort. Up till 1908 these had been mainly of the 2–8–0 type, but in the years 1908–11 a number of large Mallet compounds were put to work. The Burlington, operating westwards from Chicago over prairie country, is not gener-ally troubled by severe gradients, and the use of the 2–6–6–2 wheel arrangements, with driving wheels as large as 4 ft. 8 in. diameter is indicative of these conditions. As will be inferred from an examination of our picture the steam distribution in all four cylinders is by means of slide, rather than piston valves, and 'notching up' in both high- and low-pressure cylinders was simultaneously effected by one reversing gear. The locomotive was designed for maximum flexibility when negotiating yard layouts, and although the total wheel-base was 44 ft., the rigid wheelbase was no more than 10 ft. The cylinder diameters were $21\frac{1}{2}$ in. high pressure and 33 in. low pressure, with a common stroke of 32 in. The tractive effort was 63,300 lb. and the total engine weight was 161 tons.

148 Natal Government Railways: 2–6–6–0 Mallet Compound Freight Loco-motives.

Use of the Mallet type of articulated loco-motive had great attraction on railways having heavy gradients and sharp curva-ture, and both these physical features were present in full measure on the railways of Natal. The engine illustrated was one built by the American Locomotive Company, and was introduced in South Africa as something of an experiment. It was the prelude to the designing of locomotives of the Mallet type that were built in Scotland, by the North British Locomotive Com-pany. The American-built Mallet, with its

high-pressure cylinders driving the rear engine unit, and fed from the large pipe seen passing vertically down from the dome, had piston valves for the high-pressure cylinders, but Richardson-type balanced slide valves for the low pressure. The cylinder diameters were $17\frac{1}{2}$ in. high pressure, 28 in. low pressure, both with a stroke of 26 in. The coupled wheels were 3 ft. $9\frac{1}{2}$ in. diameter, and the boiler pressure 200 lb. per sq. in. The valve gear was Walschaerts. It will be seen that two sepa-rate sandboxes were provided, on top of the boiler, one for each engine unit. The boiler and firebox were very large, and this very powerful hill-climbing engine weighed $87\frac{1}{2}$ tons in working order. The tender, with a capacity of 9 tons of coal and 4000 gallons of water weighed a further $44\frac{1}{4}$ tons. The experience with this engine was such as to lead to the use of Mallet engines for the heaviest freight working in Natal for many years.

149 Midland Railway (LTS. Sec-tion): 4–6–4 Express Tank Engine.

Prior to its absorption by the Midland Railway, the London, Tilbury, and South-end was one of the most distinctive and smartest run of the smaller railways of Great Britain. It was primarily a commuter line, bringing vast numbers of season-ticket holders into London daily from the growing residential areas clustered around Southend. In the reverse direction, princi-pally at weekends, there was a heavy flow of day excursion business. Until the Mid-land 'take-over' the largest locomotives had been the very handsome non-super heated 4–4–2 tanks of Thomas Whitelegg's design. By superb standards of maintenance, and expert enginemanship, these loco-motives successfully worked the longest trains that could be accommodated in the platforms at the London terminal station of Fenchurch Street; but the margin in reserve was small, and on succeeding his father as Locomotive Superintendent, Robert Whitelegg designed a huge 4–6–4 tank engine. At the time there was some doubt as to whether so large an engine could be accepted over the inner-suburban part of the line, west of Barking, but Whitelegg was authorized to go ahead. Unfortunately the engines proved too heavy, and being completed after the Midland 'take-over' they were transferred elsewhere. But they were magnificent looking engines, and bore the Midland livery from the outset. The two cylinders were 20 in. diameter by 26 in. stroke; coupled wheels 6 ft. 3 in. diameter, and working pressure 160 lb. per sq. in.

150 Taff Vale Railway: 0–6–2 General Service Tank Engine.

The Taff Vale was the largest and busiest of the local railways in South Wales. Its main-line system was in the form of a Y; the 'tail' was at Cardiff and the two upper extremities led up the Rhondda Valley on the one hand, and to Merthyr Tydfil on the other. At the height of its prosperity the coal traffic was prodigious, and it was worked almost entirely with 0–6–2 type tank engines. This type also ran most of the passenger trains, though there was a number of older engines engaged on lighter duties. The 0–6–2 type was developed over the years, until the design shown in our picture was produced—an enlarged version prepared for handling the additional traffic arising from war conditions in 1914–18. Then, while much of the British export trade in coal had been lost, vast quantities were needed by the Grand Fleet, then stationed mostly at Scottish bases, and

Welsh coal had to be hauled north, instead of to the docks at Cardiff, Newport, or Barry. The new Taff Vale locomotives, six of which were built by the North British Locomotive Company during the war, had two cylinders $18\frac{1}{2}$ in. diameter by 26 in. stroke; coupled wheels 5 ft. 3 in. diameter, and a boiler pressure of 160 lb. per sq. in. In working order they weighed $70\frac{1}{2}$ tons. They were not superheated.

151 East Indian Railway: 2–6–4 Passenger Tank Engine.

The Eas tIndian Railway, as well as providing one of the major links from Calcutta to the cities in the upper valley of the Ganges, and running many long-distance express trains, operated a considerable local traffic, and for this additional engine power was needed from 1910 onwards. The East Indian, although retaining its individuality in many ways, and for some time its locomotive livery, was one of the earliest of the Indian railways to be Government-owned, and a number of the Indian standard types of locomotive were introduced. While outside cylinders were usual on the larger units, such as the 4–6–0s for express passenger, and 2–8–0 for heavy goods, a 4–4–0 for lighter passenger work, and a 0–6–0 for goods was also standardized. The East Indian 2–6–4 tank illustrated was to a large extent an adaptation of the standard 0–6–0 tender engine to a suburban tank design. The cylinders and coupled wheels were the same, though the boiler and fire box were slightly larger. The 2–6–4 tank engines had two cylinders $18\frac{1}{2}$ in. diameter by 26 in. stroke; coupled wheels 5 ft. $1\frac{1}{2}$ in. diameter, and a boiler pressure of 180 lb. per sq. in. The grate area was 27 sq. ft. against 25·6 sq. ft. on the 0–6–0. The total weight of the 2–6–4 tank engine in working order was $79\frac{1}{2}$ tons.

152 Dublin and South Eastern Railway: 4-4-2 Fast Suburban Tank Engine.

Among the quartet of notable tank engines shown in this group of illustrations, the Dublin and South Eastern 4-4-2 is of distinctive design and specialized duty. The railway was formerly known as the Dublin, Wicklow, and Wexford, and from the last years of the nineteenth century it had the important task of conveying mails landed at Kingstown, from the Irish Mail steamer, via the circuitous connecting line to Kingsbridge terminus for transference to the Cork mail. It was then that the 4-4-2 tank type was first introduced, and it was the success of the locomotives built in 1893 by Sharp, Stewart & Co. on the mails and other duties that led to the larger design illustrated. A local express train service was operated along the very picturesque coastal route between Dublin, Kingstown (now Dun Laohaire), Bray, and Greystones, and in 1911 when larger engines were needed the first of four fine new locomotives was built at the Grand Canal Street Works of the company, in Dublin. The first of them, No. 20, being completed in Coronation year was named *King George*. That fast running was intended is shown by the size of the driving wheels, 6 ft. 0 in. diameter, which was then unusual for a suburban tank engine. The cylinders were 18 in. diameter by 26 in. stroke, and the boiler pressure 175 lb. per sq. in. They were not superheated.

153 Northern Railway of France: 4-6-4 Four-cylinder Compound Express Locomotive.

In France, while the main-line companies had generally followed the lead of the Orléans in adopting the 'Pacific' type for the heaviest express passenger work, the Northern, which had achieved such outstanding success with the Du Bousquet–De Glehn 'Atlantics' seemed to have hung back from the national trend. Then, in 1911, there appeared the reason why the half-anticipated Nord-Pacific had not yet materialized. As with the 'Atlantics' at the turn of the century Monsieur Du Bousquet stepped 'streets ahead' of his colleagues on the other French railways with production of the two enormous 4-6-4 experimental compound engines. They were, however, his very last effort in locomotive design, and were completed almost at the moment of his retirement. He bequeathed them to his successor, Monsieur Asselin, at a time when the political situation on the continent of Europe was beginning to look very menacing; and though early tests showed that the capabilities of the giant new engines were quite outstanding, a great deal of testing and development work would obviously need to be done before the new type was proved sufficiently to be built in quantity, for regular service. So, unfortunately, a French design that showed the utmost promise was never developed. How the Northern Railway obtained larger engines is explained under reference 88. The magnificent 4-6-4s were De Glehn compounds. The high-pressure cylinders, $17\frac{5}{8}$ in. diameter by $25\frac{1}{8}$ in. stroke were outside, and drove the centre pair of coupled wheels, while the low-pressure cylinders, $24\frac{3}{8}$ in. diameter by $28\frac{3}{4}$ in. stroke were inside and drove on to the leading pair. All four cylinders had piston valves, actuated by separately controlled sets of Walschaerts gear. The two experimental locomotives differed in respect of the fireboxes. The particular one illustrated was built by Schneider & Co. of Creusot, and had a round-topped firebox with cross-water tubes; the second engine was built at the La Chapelle works of the railway company, and had a conventional, though very large Belpaire firebox. At the time of their construction they were the largest and heaviest locomotives in Europe. It is one of the great misfortunes of locomotive history that circumstances arose to preclude their development. Their coupled wheels were 6 ft. 8¼ in. diameter, the boiler pressure 227 lb. per sq. in., and the weight of engine alone in working order, just over 100 tons.

154 Buenos Aires and Pacific Railway: 'Pacific'-type Superheated Express Locomotive of 1910.

The Argentine railways fanning out from the great nodal city of Buenos Aires all had relatively long and level runs in the first stages of their outward journey. In fact the 'B.A.P.' had, until the construction of the Trans-Australian Railway in 1917, the distinction of the longest stretch of absolutely straight track anywhere in the world, extending for more than 250 miles. In the years before the First World War, when the majority of the Argentine railways were British-owned, they were also supplied with good quality Welsh coal, and the design of the locomotives reflected this very strikingly. For example, in the powerful 'Pacific' engine shown in our picture the grate area was only 27 sq. ft., whereas the majority of European 'Pacifics' had grates of more than 40 sq. ft. Even in England grate areas of 30 ft. or more were coming into vogue. The fine engines of this type illustrated were built by the North British Locomotive Company. The two cylinders were 21 in. diameter by 26 in. stroke; coupled wheels were 5 ft. 7 in. diameter, and the boiler pressure 150 lb. per sq. in. A high degree of superheat was used. The total weight of engine and tender in working order was 144·2 tons—a big engine for 1910, even on the 5 ft. 6 in. gauge.

155 South African Railways—Natal Section: 4–8–2 Heavy Freight Locomotive, 14th Class.

After the formation of the Union of South Africa in 1910, and the amalgamation of the former Central South African, Natal, and Cape systems into a unified railway, Mr D. A. Hendrie was appointed Chief Mechanical Engineer, and one of his first actions was to design the very powerful 4–8–2 superheater goods engine for the heavily graded Natal section. The physical features of this line have already been mentioned under reference 148, which deals with the first trials of the Mallet type of articulated engine on this section. The first order for engines of the '14th class' was for twenty, and was awarded to Robert Stephenson & Co. of Darlington. Although for no more than the 3 ft. 6 in. gauge they were then the heaviest locomotives yet built by the firm. The two cylinders were 22 in. diameter by 26 in. stroke; the coupled wheels were only 4 ft. 0 in. diameter and these proportions, in conjunction with a boiler pressure of 185 lb. per sq. in., gave a tractive effort of 41,000 lb. This immense potential capacity, for a 3 ft. 6 in. gauge engine of 1913 vintage, was backed by an exceptionally fine boiler and firebox and high-degree superheating. The total weight of engine and tender in working order was 139¾ tons.

156 Italian State Railways: Four-cylinder 'Pacific' Express Locomotive.

In the period from 1910 onwards there was an increasing trend on the railways of continental Europe to adopt very much larger engines, following the lead of France in introducing the 4–6–2 type in 1907. In Austria Karl Gölsdorf with his usual ingenuity turned the wheel arrangement round the opposite way, and in some ways obtained the 'best of both worlds', in having ample space at the rear end for a wide firebox, and the flexibility of a bogie at the front (*see* ref. 22); but on the Italian State Railways the 'Pacific' type was adopted, but with a narrow, though very long firebox. These handsome engines were of large proportions having four cylinders $17\frac{3}{4}$ in. diameter by $26\frac{3}{4}$ in. stroke; the coupled wheels were 6 ft. $7\frac{7}{8}$ in. diameter, and the boiler pressure 176 lb. per sq. in. The apparently small divergencies from the round figures of British practice resulted, of course, from the conversion of the metric sizes used in the Italian design to their English equivalents. The boiler was a very large one, with a total evaporative heating surface of 2260·5 sq. ft. and Schmidt superheater, with a further 721 sq. ft. of heating surface. A notable external feature was the very long wheelbase of the bogie giving a most elegant striding effect. These engines, of which the first examples were built by Breda, of Milan, were a great success, and the class became a standard used for many years in Italy.

157 **Great Northern Railway:** 0–6–2 Armoured Train Engine.

Experience in colonial wars at the end of the nineteenth century had convinced the British military authorities of the value of armoured trains, capable of moving high fire-power from one strategic point to another rapidly. In the early stages of the First World War attacks on the east coast of England, and indeed full-scale invasion

were considered a strong possibility. At that period in history railways were the only practicable means of transport for large numbers of troops, or heavy equipment, and in addition to making comprehensive and highly secret arrangements for the movement and deployment of men, an armoured train was built for home defence purposes. The job was divided between the Great Northern works at Doncaster, and the London and North Western works at Crewe. The latter, as by far the larger establishment, built the 'train', which consisted of a heavy bogie platform carrying the gun itself, and also heavily armoured accommodation for the crew. Doncaster took one of the standard 0–6–2 tank engines normally engaged on the London surburban service from Moorgate and King's Cross, and completely sheathed it in armour plating, giving it the queer look shown in our picture. Those 0–6–2 tanks were smart-running, ideal engines for the job, though it was never necessary for that armoured train to go into action.

158 **Great Eastern Railway:** Car for Ambulance Train, World War I.

The outbreak of war in 1914 affected the railways of Great Britain in a diversity of ways. While in the first few months every locomotive that could turn a wheel was utilized for working troops and munitions trains, immediate preparations were put in hand for the transport of wounded men who it was expected would be landed at the Channel ports in considerable numbers once the British Expeditionary Force became engaged with the enemy. At the carriage works of all the major railways of Great Britain work began, in the utmost urgency, upon converting main-line bogie corridor carriages into ambulance cars, and many complete trains were speedily made available. The Great Eastern carriage illustrated was one of a nine-coach train. Five of these coaches were originally brake-thirds. The whole of the interior was stripped out, and they were converted into ward cars, each capable of carrying twenty stretcher cases. Another car was fitted out as a pharmacy with operating theatre and all medical necessities, while two further cars provided nursing and medical staff accommodation—the personnel concerned living on the train while on duty. The ninth car was a modified first-class dining-car adapted to supply meals as necessary. That the first of these trains was ready to go anywhere within Great Britain in less than a month from the outbreak of war was a magnificent feat of organization.

159 Great Eastern Railway: 4–6–0 Express Passenger Locomotive in Wartime Livery.

Prior to the war, the Great Eastern Railway had one of the most colourful of the old styles for its locomotives, with a basic royal-blue set off by much polished brass and copper work, and a handsome lining out in red and white. Some of the British railways maintained their old colour schemes throughout the war period; but the Great Eastern changed to one of the utmost simplicity, painting all engines as they required attention in plain bluish-grey, without any lining, while the engine number was displayed in large white numerals on the tender. The locomotive shown in our picture was one of the latest express designs, introduced in 1912. They were a 4–6–0 development of the very celebrated 'Claud Hamilton' class 4–4–0, suitably enlarged, and with the important addition of superheating. The new engines were an immediate and resounding success,

and their increased haulage capacity over the 4–4–0s was of immense value during the war years when loads were greatly increased over previous standards. These engines had two cylinders 20 in. diameter by 28 in. stroke; coupled wheels 6 ft. 6 in. diameter, and a boiler pressure of 180 lb. per sq. in. By the time the Great Eastern was absorbed in the L.N.E.R. system, after grouping there were seventy of these engines at work.

160 Railway Operating Division: Ex-Midland Railway Kirtley-type 0–6–0 Goods Engine.

In the later stages in the long-drawn-out campaigns on the Western Front in the First World War, there was formed a Railway Operating Division of the British Imperial Armies, for the express purpose of transporting troops, munitions, and supplies of all kinds behind the lengthy battlefront. It was manned by British railwaymen of all grades, and commanded by the great Lt.-Col. C. W. Paget, formerly General Superintendent of the Midland Railway. Locomotives and rolling-stock were sent from England; many new locomotives were built specially. Many of the British railways sent out locomotives they could ill spare; others were of lighter and older types for which there was plenty of use on the lines behind the battlefronts. One such veteran was the Midland 0–6–0 illustrated. During the great German offensive of March 1918, in which a tremendous drive was made to capture the city of Amiens, old 2717 was a little too near to the front for safety. She was stranded in ground that became a battlefield, and was duly captured by the enemy. The Germans also needed every locomotive they could get. The British inscription 'ROD' was painted out, and her Midland number

ways of those days purchased their locomotives from a diversity of builders in
Great Britain, France, Germany, Holland,
as well as from certain Spanish firms. These
engines had more of a French rather than
an American look about them. They had
cylinders 23 in. diameter by 26 in. stroke,
and the coupled-wheel diameter was 5 ft.
9 in. The total weight of engine and tender
in working order was 131 tons. They did
good work, and except for one, that was
destroyed in the Civil War, the whole
class was in service until quite recently.

166 Northern Railway of Spain: 2-8-0 Mixed Traffic Locomotive of 1909.

The Northern Railway (Norte), as its
name suggests, ran northwards from
Madrid, and its main lines fanned out to
six termini on the coast of the Bay of
Biscay: Corunna, Aviles, Gijon, Santander,
Bilbao, and Irun, at which point connection was made with the Midi Railway of
France. The majority of these routes
involved heavy gradients. There was much
traffic of an intermediate kind, and a
'general service' 2-8-0 was an ideal
machine. It should be added that the Norte
system covered the north-eastern parts of
Spain by a series of lines making their way
eastwards from the important junction of
Miranda, on the international route to
Irun. This 2-8-0 was a solid 'work-horse'
of a locomotive, so outstandingly successful that ultimately no fewer than 436 were
in service. From 1909 when the first ten
were built, construction continued until
1943; over the years no fewer than nine
different firms received orders for successive batches of them. The design remained
virtually unchanged throughout, except

that one group of eighty engines, built
between 1938 and 1943 had Lentz poppet
valve gear. All the rest had Walschaerts.
The cylinders were 24 in. diameter by $25\frac{1}{2}$
in. stroke; the coupled wheels were 5 ft.
$1\frac{1}{2}$ in. diameter, and the total weight of
engine and tender of those with Walschaerts valve gear was 112 tons. The
engines with Lentz gear were slightly
heavier.

167 Madrid, Zaragoza and Alicante Railway: 4-8-0 Heavy Mixed Traffic Locomotive.

It is extremely interesting to study the remarkable individuality of locomotive design on most of the Spanish railways. The
gauge was different from that of France
and most of continental Europe, and the
mountain barrier of the Pyrenees seemed
to engender a degree of isolationism. At an
early date both the Western and M.Z.A.
companies, experiencing the need for
larger locomotives than 4-6-0s, adopted
the 4-8-0 type rather than the 'Pacific', for
heavy general work. This type is, of
course, far superior to the 'Pacific' for
reliable work on heavy mountain grades,
where slipping can be a great handicap;
but the Spanish railways were almost alone
among the railways of Europe in so doing.
The 4-8-0 was popular in South Africa,
but it made little headway elsewhere. It
was developed with great success in Spain.
The M.Z.A. example shown in our picture
was one of the earliest examples. The first
95 engines of the class were built in Germany by Henschel in 1912-13, and a further 25 were added to the stock after the
war in 1921. They had cylinders $22\frac{3}{4}$ in.
diameter by 26 in. stroke; the coupled
wheels were 4 ft. 7 in. diameter, and the
total weight of engine and tender in

working order was 115 tons. Their weight may seem rather small but these engines had relatively small tenders. The majority are still in service today.

168 Northern Railways of Spain: Four-cylinder Compound 'Pacific' Locomotive.

Although, as mentioned under reference 167, 'Pacifics' have always been somewhat rare in Spain, it is important to appreciate the French influence in the years before the First World War, and the very favourable impression that the working of the four-cylinder De Glehn compounds made in countries far beyond that of their origin. The fifteen engines of this class, all of which were built by the Société Alsacienne of Belfort, were supplied in two batches. The first, of six engines, in 1911, and the second lot in 1914. With coupled wheels 5 ft. 9 in. diameter they were well suited to express passenger working on the North line. The cylinder diameters were $14\frac{1}{2}$ in. high pressure and $22\frac{1}{2}$ in. low pressure, with a stroke of $25\frac{1}{4}$ in. The boiler pressure was 227 lb. per sq. in., and the total weight of engine in working order was 75 tons. Our picture shows one of them in their final form, as serving the RENFE, and generally working in their old territory, mostly north and east of Burgos. At that time they were fitted with smoke-deflecting shields on either side of the smokebox. These accessories were not deemed necessary at the time of their construction, and certainly detract from what was a very handsome outline. When first introduced these engines worked over all parts of the main line between Madrid and the French frontier. They were designed to work maximum tonnage trains at $46\frac{1}{2}$ m.p.h. on level track.

169 Western Maryland Railway: A Class 'H8' 2-8-0 Freight Locomotive of 1914.

By the outbreak of the First World War in 1914, the 2-8-0 type as a heavy freighter was coming into increasingly widespread use in Great Britain, though by that time it was being superseded by much larger types in the U.S.A. Ten-coupled locomotives were becoming common on many railways, while the development of the Mallet system of articulation was putting into service locomotives that were virtually the equivalent of two 2-8-0s in one. It is interesting, therefore, to find so important a mineral carrier as the Maryland putting new 2-8-0s on the road as relatively late as 1914. The main line extends for 258 miles from Baltimore to Connellsville, where it made an end-on junction with the New York Central for the last 58 miles of the run to Pittsburgh. It is true that in crossing the Allegheny Mountains very large Mallet locomotives were used; but east of Cumberland the *average* revenue tonnage—not the gross load—of freight trains handled by the 'H8' engines illustrated was 657 tons. The maximum loads handled unassisted by these remarkable engines was 7000 tons. They had two cylinders 25 in. diameter by 30 in. stroke; coupled wheels of 4 ft. 4 in. diameter, and a tractive effort of 61,300 lb. The total weight of engine only was 109 tons. They represent one of the highest developments of the 2-8-0 type anywhere in the world.

170 Commonwealth Railways, Australia: 2-8-0 Standard Freight Locomotive.

The completion of the great transcontinental line between Port Augusta and Kalgoorlie in 1917 was one of the greatest romances of relatively modern railway construction. The adoption of the 4 ft. 8½ in. gauge, sandwiched between the 3 ft. 6 in. gauge of Western Australia and the 5 ft. 3 in. of South Australia has only just 'paid off' in the completion, in 1970, of a line on the 4 ft. 8½ in. gauge right across Australia. But in 1917 the 'Trans', as it is generally known 'down under', was isolated from the other 4 ft. 8½ in. gauge lines, and it had to be self-contained. For working the 1100-mile line across what was virtually continuous desert country, standard New South Wales locomotive types were adopted, and the first supplies had to come from Great Britain. They were needed in great urgency in the middle of the war, and the North British Locomotive Company built eight 2–8–0s of standard New South Wales design for the freight traffic. These excellent and magnificently reliable engines had cylinders 22 in. diameter by 26 in. stroke; coupled wheels 4 ft. 3 in. diameter, and a boiler pressure of 150 lb. per sq. in. They had large tenders to carry them for long runs in most inhospitable country, and engine and tender in working order weighed 116 tons.

171 **Paris, Lyons, and Mediterranean Railway:** Four-cylinder Compound 2–8–2 built in the U.S.A.

The immense manufacturing capacity of the famous Baldwin Locomotive Works, could not be exemplified better than by the large additional orders they were able to undertake during the First World War. Under reference 163 the special 2–8–0s for use of the American armies in Europe are illustrated, and at the same time as an astonishing rate of productivity was being maintained in the supply of these engines the Works was not only building similar

ones for the British Government but turning large numbers of compound freight 2–8–2s of a wholly French design—all this, of course, additional to the normal work of supplying the American home railways. The French compound 2–8–2s illustrated were of standard P.L.M. design originating in 1914, and in their numerous refinements of detail were in strong contrast to the tough, starkly-simple 2–8–0s in production for traffic immediately leading up to the American sectors of the long battle-line of the Western Front. The compound 2–8–2s were of the standard P.L.M. type of cylinder arrangement, which was the reverse of the De Glehn system. The high-pressure cylinders were inside driving the second pair of coupled wheels and the low pressure outside driving the third pair. The high-pressure cylinders were 20 in. diameter by 25⅝ in. stroke; the low pressure, 28¾ in. diameter by 27⅝ in. stroke. The coupled-wheel diameter was 5 ft. 5 in., and the boiler pressure 227 lb. per sq. in. The designed performance was the haulage of 1300-ton freight trains at a speed of 28 m.p.h.

172 **Swiss Federal Railways:** 2–10–0 Four-cylinder Compound for the Gotthard Section.

Under reference 143 a description is given of a powerful 2–8–0 freight engine for the Gotthard line, and the arduous conditions of service existing there were emphasized. At the end of the year, 1913, some still more powerful freight engines were delivered from the Swiss Locomotive Works at Winterthur. These, as shown in the present picture, were of the 2–10–0 type, and they were interesting as representing a breakaway from the settled policy of using compound propulsion. Of the five new engines, three were compounds and two, of otherwise identical proportions and power, were four-cylinder simples. The compounds, of which one is shown in our picture, had high-pressure cylinders $18\frac{1}{2}$ in. diameter, and low pressure, 28 in. diameter. The stroke in both was $25\frac{1}{4}$ in. The simples had four cylinders of the same size as the high-pressure cylinders of the compounds; the coupled-wheel diameter on both groups of locomotives was 4 ft. $4\frac{3}{8}$ in. The working conditions were not quite equal in that the compounds had a boiler pressure of 216 lb. per sq. in. and the simples 186 lb. per sq. in. The simples had slightly larger superheaters. The eventual outcome of this comparison is not widely known, because the war years followed, and not long afterwards, in 1922, the Gotthard line was converted to electric traction.

173 **London and North Western Railway:** The War Memorial 4-6-0 Engine, No. 1914 *Patriot*.

Until the year 1916 every express passenger locomotive on the London and North Western Railway was named: large and small, ancient and modern alike. And an immense variety of names was used. There was little system about it. As older engines were scrapped the names were handed down to new ones being constructed. Great events and great personalities were honoured; during the First World War engines were named after Allied leaders, great battles, railway ships lost in war service, but from 1916 onwards the need to economize in the use of brass led to a temporary end to engine naming. Then when the war was over, although naming was not generally resumed, the first of a new batch of four-cylinder 4-6-0 express passenger engines of the 'Claughton' class was

specially named, as a kind of mobile war memorial. It had a specially large name-plate bearing the inscription:

PATRIOT
In memory of the fallen
L. & N.W.R. employees, 1914–1919

The number, 1914, was already borne by another engine; but this was changed, so that *Patriot* could have the number 1914. The new engine, completed at Crewe Works in 1920 became the pride of the line, and for many months continuously worked the afternoon Anglo-Scottish express from Euston as far as Crewe. The 'Claughton' class, of which *Patriot* was the newest member, dated from 1913. They had four cylinders $15\frac{3}{4}$ in. diameter by 26 in. stroke; 6 ft. 9 in. coupled wheels; a boiler pressure of 175 lb. per sq. in., and the tractive effort was 24,500 lb. *Patriot* was the sixty-first engine of the class, which eventually was 130 strong.

174 **Great Central Railway:** The War Memorial Engine, No. 1165 *Valour*.

It was not until the introduction of the *Sir Sam Fay* class 4-6-0 (ref. 45), that the Great Central Railway began the systematic naming of all its new express passenger locomotives. In 1918 a very large four-cylinder version of the *Sir Sam Fay* was completed at Gorton Works in 1918, and named after the chairman of the company, *Lord Faringdon*. When some further engines of this same class were built after the war the Great Central followed the lead of the London and North Western in specifying one of these large and handsome engines as a 'War Memorial', and in 1920 No. 1165 was named *Valour*, and given a special inscription: 'In memory of G.C.R. Employees who Gave their Lives for their

Country 1914–18. Unlike the North Western engine *Patriot*, which was dressed in 'mourning' to the extent even of suppressing the red background to the number-plates, the Great Central engine was decked, as it were, in a warrior's full-dress uniform, in all the magnificent colouring standard on the express passenger engines. Unfortunately, although the names and the special plates with their inscriptions survived for many years, the significance of the painting passed with the grouping of the railways. *Patriot* was ultimately painted in Midland red, and renumbered 5964, while *Valour* assumed the standard L.N.E.R. apple-green, which was a simplified version of the old Great Northern style. The leading dimensions of *Valour* were: cylinders (four) 16 in. diameter by 26 in. stroke; coupled wheels 6 ft. 9 in. diameter; boiler pressure 180 lb. per sq. in.

175 **London, Brighton, and South Coast Railway:** 'Dedication' Locomotive, No. 333 *Remembrance*.

At the very end of its independent existence the London, Brighton, and South Coast Railway put in hand a further five express passenger locomotives of its successful 4–6–4 tank type, and the first of the new engines took the road early in 1922. During the nineteenth century engine naming on the Brighton line had been so general that everything except the ordinary goods engines were named, even including the local, suburban tank engines. But when D. Earle-Marsh succeeded R. J. Billinton, naming of all engines virtually ceased, except for one or two special cases. The first of the new 4–6–4 tanks of 1922 was named *Stephenson*. It was finished in the standard chocolate-brown livery, and was followed by three more engines of the

same design, but all unnamed. Then the last engine of the series, No. 333, was specified as a 'Dedication' locomotive. Although having the standard black-and-white lining a livery of plain grey replaced the chocolate-brown; it was named *Remembrance* and carried a bronze memorial tablet on the tank sides with the inscription: 'In grateful remembrance of the 532 men of the L.B. & S.C. Rly. who gave their lives for their country, 1914–1919.' *Remembrance* took the road after the Brighton railway had become a part of the Southern system, in January 1923; and like her counterparts on the L. & N.W.R. and the Great Central she did not bear her significant painting style for very long. In the standard olive-green of early Southern days the name was rendered on a cast brass-plate, instead of the old Brighton style, and this surmounted the original memorial placques.

176 **Great Indian Peninsular Railway:** War Memorial 4–6–0 Express Locomotive, *Hero*.

The last of the 'War Memorial' locomotives to be mentioned here is that of the Great Indian Peninsula Railway. As in the case of the three British companies the locomotives of which are shown on these pages, the G.I.P.R. example is one of a standard type, similar to previous engines of the 4–6–0 type introduced on to the railway since the early 1900s. It was one of a series built by the Vulcan Foundry in 1921, and its special name-plate bears the inscription: 'In memory of G.I.P. Railway employees who gave their lives in the Great War 1914–1918.' Technically it was a straightforward two-cylinder simple with cylinders $20\frac{1}{2}$ in. diameter by 26 in. stroke; coupled wheels 6 ft. 2 in. diameter, and a boiler pressure of 160 lb. per sq. in. These engines were arranged for oil firing, as originally supplied, but adapted so as to be easily converted to coal-burning if required. Although this 4–6–0 design follows that of various other Indian railways on the 5 ft. 6 in. gauge the G.I.P.R. retained various small marks of its own individuality, such as the well-known chocolate-brown livery and stovepipe chimneys.

177 Belfast and County Down Railway: 4–6–4 Express Tank Engine.

This compact little system, completely described geographically by its name, operated two 'residential' lines to the east of Belfast, and a semi-main-line running southwards to Downpatrick, there forking to serve two lines to coastal termini at Newcastle and Ardglass. The whole system as operating in the years just before the First World War was no more than 80 miles long, and had then a stock of no more than thirty locomotives. But the residential traffic was always on the increase, with daily commuters tending to live further from Belfast; and after the war the need was felt for more powerful locomotives. The traffic was ideal for tank engines, and the Locomotive Superintendent, J. L. Crosthwait, designed a very handsome class of 4–6–4 tank engines, which were built by Beyer, Peacock & Co. Ltd. They were the first engines of this type to run on one of the broad-gauge (5 ft. 3 in.) sections of the Irish railways. It is interesting to recall also that Mr Crosthwait, like his contemporary E. Sharples on the Furness Railway, did not consider it necessary to have superheaters on these short-run 4–6–4 tanks. Apart from the use of outside cylinders and Walschaerts valve gear these B.C.D.R. 4–6–4s were very similar in general capacity to the Furness 4–6–4s. Crosthwait's 4–6–4s had two cylinders 19 in. diameter by 26 in. stroke; 5 ft. 3 in. coupled wheels; a boiler pressure of 170 lb. per sq. in., and a tractive effort of 20,550 lb. The total weight in working order was 81·6 tons.

178 London and South Western Railway: The Urie 'N.15' Class 4–6–0 Express Passenger Engine of 1918.

Robert Urie, who became Chief Mechanical Engineer of the L.S.W.R. in 1912, had worked with the great Dugald Drummond for a very large part of his life, first on the Caledonian Railway, and then as Locomotive Works Manager on the L.S.W.R. That did not, however, mean that Urie had accepted all of his former chief's precepts. Far from it! So far as large express passenger locomotives the extremely simple 'N15' class of 1918, the subject of our picture, could not present a much stronger contrast to the latest and largest of Drummond's 4–6–0s. Instead of the use of four cylinders, with much machinery between the frames, Urie used two cylinders only, with outside Walschaerts valve gear, and everything readily accessible from outside. These engines followed in a tradition that Urie was in process of establishing on the London and South Western Railway, and which eventually became a British standard after nationalization of the railways in 1948. Apart from the layout of their machinery the Urie 'N15' 4–6–0s of 1918 were magnificently built in what could be termed the 'Scottish tradition' brought south by Dugald Drummond, and carried on by many Scottish engineers who followed him to the L.S.W.R. The cylinders were 22 in. diameter by 28 in. stroke; coupled-wheel diameter of 6 ft. 7 in., and a boiler pressure of 180 lb. per sq. in. After grouping they were developed by R. E. L. Maunsell into the outstandingly successful 'King Arthur' class of the Southern Railway.

179 **Highland Railway:** The 'Clan' Class 4–6–0 Express Passenger Locomotive.

The establishment of the main base of the British 'Grand Fleet' at Scapa Flow in the Orkney Islands for the whole of the First World War threw an immensely increased traffic upon the Highland Railway. In normal times the traffic was seasonal, and the quiet periods during the winter enabled repair and maintenance work to be carried out on the bulk of the locomotive stock, so as to have available practically the entire stock for the heavy summer tourist season. During the war, although the tourist business vanished, the naval traffic was continuous all the year round, and the Highland Railway found itself with not enough locomotives to do the job. Some were borrowed from other companies; a limited number of new ones were purchased, but it was not until the very end of the war that new engines of Mr Cumming's design began to come into service. The first four of the new 'Clan' class, built by R. W. Hawthorn, Leslie & Co., of Newcastle, took the road in time for the late summer traffic of 1919. They were extremely robust, free-steaming, and generally reliable engines, ideally suited to the hard work involved with heavy mail and passenger trains over the severe gradients of the Highland line. The first four were painted in the dark green livery shown in our picture, but a further batch put into traffic in 1922 carried a very pleasing shade of pale leaf green. The two cylinders were 21 in. diameter by 26 in.

stroke; coupled wheels 6 ft. 0 in. diameter, and a boiler pressure of 170 lb. per sq. in. After grouping, all eight engines of the class were transferred to the Callander and Oban line of the former Caledonian Railway where they did extremely good work until the outbreak of the Second World War.

180 **Great Southern and Western Railway:** Four-cylinder 4–6–0 Express Passenger Locomotive.

When R. E. L. Maunsell left the G.S. & W.R. in 1913 to become Chief Mechanical Engineer of the South Eastern and Chatham Railway, E. A. Watson was appointed to succeed him at Inchicore. Watson had received some of his earlier experience at Swindon, Great Western Railway, and he had become a great admirer of the locomotive practice of G. J. Churchward. There was certainly a need for more powerful locomotives for the Dublin–Cork main-line service, and Watson set the Inchicore drawing office on to the design of a four-cylinder 4–6–0 with a basic capacity comparable to that of Churchward's 'Star' class (ref. 74). The 'engine' layout was similar, with the outside cylinders driving the centre pair of coupled wheels, and the inside pair set well forward, to drive the leading pair. The valve gear was Walschaerts, but, in contrast to Swindon practice, arranged outside. The boiler, also, was of a more conventional design than Churchward's famous tapered-barrel type, and carried a pressure of 175 lb. per sq. in. against the Great Western 225. The four cylinders of the Irish engine were 14 in. diameter by 26 in. stroke, and coupled-wheel diameter was 6 ft. 7 in. These dimensions provided a tractive effort of 19,850 lb. In detail design these engines showed a number of defects, particularly in the steam circuit; and although capable of a good turn of speed it was found necessary later to rebuild them with a simplified cylinder layout, with two cylinders only, outside.

181 Great Eastern Railway: Signal Gantry at Stratford.

In the years of railway pre-eminence in England signalling practice, in respect of the indications given to locomotive drivers, did not change a great deal, and a striking feature of the railway scene was the large number of signal gantries carrying many small posts—'doll' posts as they were known—each in turn with a large number of semaphore arms. Successful operation of the traffic depended to a large extent upon the road knowledge of the driver. When faced with a configuration such as that in our picture the driver had to interpret what he saw, and act accordingly. The situation might appear to be very confusing to a lay-man, but actually it was not so complicated or confusing as it might at first sight be imagined. This particular gantry, on the Great Eastern main line, situated about four miles from the London terminus of Liverpool Street, provides a very good example. There are six running lines, three in each direction passing beneath the gantry, and the posts on the gantry are arranged in three distinct groups. The situation is made more clear by the large sign THROUGH applied to the centre group. It was at one time customary to refer to the principal, or main lines, as the 'through' lines, others being local, or otherwise designated. At the junctions immediately ahead one could proceed on any one of five routes from each of the three running lines in the direction proceeding away from the artist, and the significance of the various alternative routes is indicated by the heights and geographical location of the semaphore arms on the posts. For example, express passenger trains proceeding on the main or 'through' line would be signalled by the uppermost of the group of semaphores in the centre group. If a train was running on the through line under the gantry, and was required to diverge either to the right or left, or proceed into the sidings that exist further down the line the appropriate semaphores would be lowered. Drivers from their road knowledge would know instantly what was required of them: whether by day, when the complete array of semaphores could be seen, or by night, when a corresponding display of lights would be seen.

182 Central Railways of Brazil: Elevated Signal Box and Signal Bridge.

In localities where track circuiting was not installed, it was essential for signalmen to have a clear view of all the tracks over which their signals controlled train movements. Actually track circuits were very much the exception rather than the rule in most parts of the world, Great Britain included. Considerable ingenuity was shown in many locations to give signalmen a good view of tracks, and in many places the box was built on an elevated structure overhanging, or actually spanning the tracks. Our picture shows a fine example of a British-built signal-box carried on a gantry structure at the terminal station of the Central Railway of Brazil in Rio de Janeiro. The design of the installation, and the type of signals, are wholly British with lower-quadrant semaphore arms, and shorter arms below the main running signals for controlling shunting movements. The signals are mounted on the same gantry as the signal-box, and include signals for outgoing as well as ingoing traffic. While this arrangement made things favourable for the observances of traffic the engineering implications were considerable. The signals mounted on the gantry were far from the only ones required for working the station, and there was a great number of points. The wires for signal operation and all the point rodding had to be carried to one end of the gantry or the other, and then led through appropriate cranks and vertically-guided rodding down the main end-supports of the gantry to lead-offs at ground level. This was quite an outstanding example of mechanical engineering.

183 **Canadian Northern Railway:** 'Pacific' Type Express Passenger Locomotive.

This line provided some of the most important western routes of what is now the Canadian National Railway system, and in 1914, there were almost 4700 miles of route under ownership of the C.N.R. in western Canada. Furthermore, there were associated companies in the Eastern Provinces carrying the Canadian Northern connections as far east as Nova Scotia. At the time of the outbreak of war, in 1914, a line to rival the Canadian Pacific through the 'Rockies' was under construction from Edmonton, Alberta, through the Yellowhead Pass to reach the canyons of the Fraser River, and so to Vancouver. For the long passenger hauls over the prairie divisions the 'Pacific' type of locomotive was used. One can say that it was a very typical example of heavy passenger locomotive in North America just before the war, just as

the Canadian Pacific 4-6-2 (ref. 185) was typical of the immediate post-war period. The Canadian Northern locomotive illustrated had two cylinders 23 in. diameter by 28 in. stroke; coupled wheels of 5 ft. 9 in. diameter, and used a boiler pressure of 170 lb. per sq. in. The tractive effort was 30,600 lb. A special feature of these locomotives was the very large firebox, with a grate area of 48·2 sq. ft. This was designed to use low-grade soft coal. The typical bell, mounted on the boiler between the chimney and the sandbox was actuated by a steam-operated bell-ringer. The total weight of engine and tender in working order was $154\frac{1}{2}$ tons.

184 **New York Central System:** 'Pacific' Type Express Passenger Locomotive.

The New York Central and Hudson River Railroad gradually extended its activities from a main line running precisely in accordance with its name to a 'group' stretching as far west as Chicago. Over its tracks were operated, even before 1914, such famous trains as the Empire State Express and the Twentieth Century Limited. The route being of a water-level nature involved no long, nor severe gradients, and it became the tradition to operate very heavy trains. The coaching stock then used was also, in relation to its accommodation, very heavy, and an eleven-coach train could weigh at least 800 tons. Through the suburbs of New York the trains were electrically hauled, and then the next 135 miles, to Albany, was booked to be run in 160 minutes, an average of just over 50 m.p.h. The 'Pacific' type of locomotive shown in our picture was used for this kind of work. The New York Central used locomotives that appeared to have a relatively low tractive effort; but they were steamed continuously very hard, and had very efficient boilers and fireboxes, with a high degree of superheat in the steam. On paper this N.Y.C. 4–6–2, with cylinders $23\frac{1}{2}$ in. diameter and 26 in. stroke, and coupled wheels as large as 6 ft. 7 in. diameter, appears to be considerably less powerful than the Canadian Northern 4–6–2 (ref. 183); but in general the work they were called upon to do was consistently harder.

185 Canadian Pacific Railway: 4–6–2 Type Express Passenger Locomotive.

It is no exaggeration to say that the Canadian Pacific is one of the most famous railways in the world. A lifeline of national development in Canada itself, with its steamship interests, it held at one time the unique position of providing through communication from Great Britain westwards to the 'Far East' by the ships and trains of one administration. The railway itself is one of markedly varying characteristics, with the long level stretches across the prairies contrasting strongly with the exceedingly mountainous sections through the Rockies. In 1919 some very fine new 'Pacific' engines were introduced for the fast-running sections of line, east of Winnipeg and for the very important inter-city service between Montreal and Toronto. These locomotives were built at the Angus Works of the company in Montreal, and although of an entirely new design a high rate of productivity was achieved in their construction, attaining an output of one of these large engines every $5\frac{1}{2}$ working days. They were the largest and heaviest locomotives to run on any line in Canada. They were extremely simple in the layout of their machinery, with two huge cylinders

25 in. diameter by 30 in. stroke; coupled wheels 6 ft. 3 in. diameter, and a boiler pressure of 200 lb. per sq. in. The tractive effort was 42,000 lb. The total weight of engine and tender in working order was 215 tons. They were very successful in service, and paved the way for later developments towards the 4–6–4 'Hudson' type on the Canadian Pacific Railway.

186 Missouri Pacific Railroad: Medium-weight 4–8–2 Mixed Traffic Locomotive.

This railroad had its origins in one of the earliest lines in the Middle West of the U.S.A., having been formed in 1849 to build a 'Pacific Railroad' to extend from St Louis via Jefferson City to the western boundary of Missouri and thence through to the Pacific seaboard. It never reached the Pacific. Like several other railroads its fortunes became involved in the Civil War, and in 1872 it went bankrupt. Subsequent changes and amalgamations produced the present company, which although owning nearly 10,000 route miles of track does not extend farther west than Pueblo, Colorado, where it links up with the Denver and Rio Grande Western. It is, therefore, a line of the prairie and wheatlands of the Middle West, and required locomotives of less power than of those passing through the mountain ranges of the Rockies. Shortly after the First World War the railroad took delivery of thirty new eight-coupled main-line locomotives. Twenty-five of these were of the 2–8–2 type, but five, of which one is illustrated, were of the 4–8–2, or Mountain type. It was interesting to find this wheel arrangement used at a relatively early date because its potentialities could not be fully realized until the introduction of mechanical stokers, when the large fireboxes could be fed at a sufficient rate to raise steam, to develop the *nominal* tractive effort of the locomotive to a reality. In later years the Missouri Pacific developed the '5308' class into an extremely powerful and effective unit; but this lies several years ahead of the period covered by this book.

187 South Australian Railways: The Mighty '700' Class 2–8–2.

Until the end of 1922 the locomotive policy of the South Australian Railways had been virtually stagnant for a number of years. Engineers had been rather overawed by the low limit of axle-loading permitted, even on the 5 ft. 3 in. gauge main lines. But the appointment of W. A. Webb as Commissioner of Railways in the State in 1922 changed everything. He demanded the introduction of much larger engines, to eliminate the double-heading that had become necessary with all heavy trains crossing the Mount Lofty Range, and equally demanded the improvement in permanent way that would permit of an increase in maximum axle-load on the main line, from 18 to 23½ tons. He was fortunate in having as Chief Mechanical Engineer F. J. Shea, a relatively young man, with experience of locomotive working in the U.S.A. He designed two huge new locomotives, one of the 4–8–2 and the other of the 2–8–2 type, distinctly American in appearance, but wholly Australian in conception. The first examples of each class were built in England by Sir W. G. Armstrong-Whitworth & Co., of Newcastle. Our picture shows one of the 2–8–2s as originally delivered, and its great size caused a positive sensation when it was unloaded from the ship at Port Adelaide. The two cylinders were 22 in. diameter by 28 in. stroke;

coupled wheels 4 ft. 9 in. diameter, and a boiler pressure of 200 lb. per sq. in. Total weight of engine and tender in working order was no less than 171 tons, and the tractive effort was 40,400 lb. The type was later developed into a colossal 2–8–4, with booster, in the early 1930s.

188 Great Northern Railway (England) The Gresley 'Pacific' Locomotive.

It is appropriate to conclude the story of this period with an illustration of one of the first of these celebrated locomotives of 1922, because they marked very clearly the beginning of a new era of locomotive design in Great Britain. It was the era of really large boilers. Hitherto great ingenuity had been shown by many locomotive designers in producing boilers that were relatively high steam-raisers, when in favourable circumstances of working, with good coal, expert management, and carefully regulated rosters and maintenance routines. But the First World War and the periods of labour troubles that had followed it had shown a different side of railway working, and H. N. Gresley, in designing a six-coupled express locomotive, provided what was then an enormous boiler for Great Britain. On the grouping of the railways in 1923, Gresley was appointed Chief Mechanical Engineer of the London and North Eastern, and his 'Pacifics' became the standard express locomotives for heavy main-line working. It was some years before the other railways began to follow Gresley's example, so far as boilers were concerned. A surviving locomotive of this class, the *Flying Scotsman*, made extensive tours of the U.S.A. in 1969 and 1970. The 'Pacifics' had the arrangement of three cylinders and valve gear as on the 'Mogul' engines (ref. 120). They had three cylinders, 20 in. diameter by 26 in. stroke; coupled-wheel diameter of 6 ft. 8 in.; a boiler pressure of 180 lb. per sq. in., and a tractive effort of 29,835 lb. Some important improvements were made to the valve setting in 1927, as a result of which they became increasingly efficient, and very free running. A later development of this same basic design, but with higher boiler pressure, reached a maximum speed of 108 m.p.h. in 1935.

BIBLIOGRAPHY

BOOKS

L. M. Vilain, *Les locomotives à vapeur Françaises du 'Type Pacific'*, Vigot Frères, Paris, 1959

L. G. Marshall, *Steam on the R.E.N.F.E.*, Macmillan, 1965

O. S. Nock, *Locomotives of Sir Nigel Gresley*, Longmans Green, 1945

O. S. Nock, *Locomotives of R. E. L. Maunsell*, Edward Everard, Bristol, 1954

O. S. Nock, '*The Premier Line*', Ian Allan, 1952

Beyer-Garratt Locomotives, Beyer, Peacock & Co. Ltd.

The Vulcan Locomotive Works: 1830–1930, Locomotive Publishing Co. Ltd.

North British Locomotive Co. Ltd.: War 1914–19, N. B. Locomotive Co. Ltd., Glasgow

Locomotives, Robert Stephenson & Hawthorns Ltd., 1947

A. W. Bruce, *The Steam Locomotive in America*, W.W. Norton & Co. Inc., New York, 1953

PERIODICALS

The Railway Magazine, IPC Business Press Ltd.

The Locomotive Magazine, Locomotive Publishing Co. Ltd.

Baldwin Locomotives

INDEX

	Ref. No.	Page No. Description

ANIMALS

Arabian
Hump shunting	65	134

English
Collecting dog, 'Buller', at Euston	63	133
The Port Carlisle *Dandy* horse	64	133

CARRIAGES

Argentinian
Buenos Aires Pacific, family saloon	43–4	124

Australian
Victorian Railways, first-class suburban car	60	132

British
Great Central, teak-bodied bogie corridor carriage	110	153
Great Eastern, car for ambulance train, World War I	158	173
Great Northern, Gresley articulated twin carriage	109	152
London Brighton & South Coast, first-class Pullman	139	165
London Brighton & South Coast, parlour saloon interior	140	165
London Brighton & South Coast, inspection saloon	81	140
London & North Western, observation car	83	141
Midland Railway, elliptical-roofed main-line composite carriage	111	153
North British, the horse-drawn Port Carlisle *Dandy*	64	133
North Eastern, first-class dining car	137–8	164
North Wales Narrow Gauge, bogie-brake-composite carriage	16	113
South Eastern & Chatham, Pullman car	41–2	123–4

Chinese
Shanghai–Nanking, third-class composite brake and mail van	59	131

Indian
Bengal Nagpur & G.I.P. Joint, first- and second-class composite carriage	61	132
Maharajah of Rewar, private train saloon	82	141

Turkish
Ottoman, first-class saloon carriage	62	132

LEVEL CROSSINGS

British
Crossing gates	115	155
Wicket gates	116	155

U.S.A.
The 'Union' Automatic Flagman	112	154

LOCOMOTIVES

Argentinian
Buenos Aires and Pacific, superheated express, 1910	154	172

	Ref. No.	Page No. Description

Australian

Commonwealth Railways, 2–8–0 standard freight	170	178
South Australian, the mighty '700' class 2–8–2	187	187
Tasmanian Government, express 4–4–2 and 2–4–4 Garratt	49	126
Victorian Railways, 4–6–2 suburban tank engine	25	117
Victorian Railways, 'A2' class 4–6–0 express passenger	101	149
Victorian Railways, 'C' class heavy freight 2–8–0	104	150

Austrian

Two-cylinder compound 4–4–0	3	108
Golsdorf's Masterpiece 2–6–4 express	22	116

Belgian

2–10–0 heavy freight locomotive	7	109

Brazilian

Central Railway, 0–6–6–0 Mallet articulated compound	145	168
San Paulo, 'Pacific'-type express passenger	86	142
San Paulo, 2–8–0 freight locomotives	136	164

British

Caledonian, McIntosh 2–6–0 express goods	118	156
Furness, 4–4–0 express passenger	24	117
Glasgow & South Western, Drummond 4–4–0	34	120
Glasgow & South Western, 4-cylinder 4–4–0 Lord Glenarthur	128	160
Great Central, Robinson 2–8–0 heavy mineral	10	111
Great Central, the Sir Sam Fay 4–6–0	45	125
Great Central, 3-cylinder 0–8–4 tank engine	52	128
Great Central, the War memorial engine, Valour	174	180
Great Eastern, 4–6–0 express passenger in wartime	159	174
Great Northern, 'Vulcan' 4-cylinder compound 'Atlantic'	4	108
Great Northern, 4–2–2 engine on 20-ton bogie well wagon	78	139
Great Northern, 0–6–2 armoured train	157	173
Great Northern, '1000' class 3-cylinder 2–6–0	120	157
Great Northern, the Gresley 'Pacific'	188	187
Great Western, 4–6–0 for Edward VII's Funeral	74	137
Great Western, 0–6–0 fast mixed traffic	117	155
Highland, the 'Clan' class 4–6–0 express passenger	179	183
Lancashire & Yorkshire, 4–4–0 superheated express passenger	89	144
Lancashire & Yorkshire, 4-cylinder 4–6–0 express passenger	48	126
London Brighton & South Coast, 4–4–2 tank engine for Royal Train	77	138
London Brighton & South Coast, 2–6–0 fast goods	119	156
London Brighton & South Coast, Dedication locomotive, Remembrance	175	181
London & North Western, 'George the Fifth' class 4–4–0 express passenger	125	159
London & North Western, War memorial engine, Patriot	173	180
London & South Western, Drummond 'D15' class 4–4–0	36	121
London & South Western, Urie 'N15' class 4–6–0 express passenger, 1918	178	182
Midland, 4–4–0 express (Royal Train)	76	138

	Ref. No.	Page No. Description
Midland, '999' class 4–4–0 express passenger	127	160
Midland (L.T.S. section) 4–6–4 express tank engine	149	169
North British, the 'REID' 'Atlantic' express passenger	91	144
North Eastern, the 'R1' class 4–4–0	1	107
North Eastern, 4–4–4 3-cylinder express tank engine	90	144
Ravenglass & Eskdale, 15-inch gauge 'Atlantic', *Sanspareil*	18	114
Somerset & Dorset Joint, 4–4–0 express passenger	33	120
South Eastern & Chatham, Wainwright 'D' class 4–4–0 express	35	121
Taff Vale, 0–6–2 general service tank engine	150	170

Bulgarian

| State Railways, 2–8–0 4-cylinder compound freight | 141 | 166 |

Canadian

| Canadian Northern, 'Pacific' type express passenger | 183 | 185 |
| Canadian Pacific, 4–6–2 express passenger | 185 | 186 |

Chilean

| State Railways, 4–6–0 express passenger, 1913 | 142 | 166 |

Chinese

| Shanghai–Nanking 'Atlantic' express passenger | 47 | 126 |
| Government Railways, 'Atlantic' express, Taokow–Chingua line | 102 | 149 |

Danish

| State Railways, 3-cylinder 4–6–0 superheated express passenger | 96 | 147 |

Dutch

| Netherlands Central, 4-cylinder 4–6–0 express | 19 | 114 |
| Netherlands State, 4-cylinder 4–6–0 express passenger | 92 | 145 |

Egyptian

| State Railways, superheated 'Atlantic' express | 87 | 143 |
| State Railways, 4–6–0 express passenger | 134 | 163 |

French

Northern Railway, 4-cylinder compound 'Pacific'	88	143
Northern Railway, 4-cylinder 4–6–4 compound express	153	171
Paris–Orléans, 4-cylinder compound 'Pacific'	66	134
P.L.M., 4-cylinder compound 'Pacific', 1909	68	135
P.L.M., 4-cylinder compound 2–8–2, American-built	171	179
State Railways, 4-cylinder compound 'Pacific'	162	175
State Railways, 2–8–0 heavy freight	161	175
Western Railways, 4-cylinder compound 'Pacific', 1908	67	135

Germany

Bavarian State, 0–8–8–0 Mallet compound tank engine	144	167
Prussian State, 4-cylinder compound 'Atlantic' express	5	108
Prussian State, 4-cylinder simple express passenger 4–6–0	21	115

Hungarian

| State Railways, 2–4–4–0 Mallet compound freight | 20 | 115 |

Indian

East Indian, 2–6–4 passenger tank engine	151	170
Great Indian Peninsular Railway, Royal Train 4–4–0 express	75	138
Great Indian Peninsular Railway, War Memorial 4–6–0 *Hero*	176	181

	Ref. No.	Page No. Description
Madras, 4–4–0 express passenger and mail	98	148
North Western, heavy goods 2–8–0	8	100
Irish		
Ballycastle, 4–4–2 tank engine, 1908	15	113
Belfast & County Down, 4–6–4 express tank engine	177	182
Dublin & South Eastern, 4–4–2 fast suburban tank engine	152	171
Great Northern, superheated 4–4–0 express	99	148
Great Southern & Western, 4–6–0 heavy goods and mixed traffic	135	163
Great Southern & Western, 4-cylinder 4–6–0 express passenger	180	183
Midland Railway (Northern Counties Committee), 4–4–0 super- heated express	100	148
West Clare, 4–6–0 tank engine, *Kilkee*, of 1909	17	114
Italian		
State Railways, 4-cylinder 'Pacific' express	156	172
Malayan		
Johore State, 'Pacific' type express passenger	85	142
New Zealand		
Government Railways, 'Ab' class express passenger 'Pacific'	103	150
Norwegian		
State Railways, 2–8–0 freight, American-built, 1919	94	146
State Railways, 2–6–2 suburban tank engine	95	146
Servian		
State Railways, 0–10–0 2-cylinder compound freight	133	162
South African		
Natal Government Railways, 2–6–6–0 Mallet compound	148	169
South African Railways, 'Pacific' type express passenger	46	125
South African Railways, Natal section, 4–8–2 heavy freight, 14th class	155	172
Spanish		
M.Z.A., American-built 4–6–2 express passenger	165	176
M.Z.A., 4–8–0 heavy mixed traffic	167	177
Northern, 2–8–0 mixed traffic, 1909	166	177
Northern, 4-cylinder compound 'Pacific'	168	178
Swedish		
State Railways, superheated 'Atlantic' type express	93	145
Swiss		
Federal Railways, 2-cylinder compound 4–4–0 express	97	147
Federal Railways, 2–10–0 4-cylinder compound for the Gotthard section	172	179
Gotthard, 2–8–0 4-cylinder compound freight	143	167
U.S.A.		
American Army in Europe 1918, 2–8–0 war service in France	163	175
Baltimore & Ohio, Class 'A3' 'Atlantic', 1910	6	109
Chicago, Burlington & Quincy, 2–6–6–2 Mallet compound, 1909	147	168
Chicago, Milwaukee & St Paul Vauclain compound 'Atlantic'	2	107
Chicago, Milwaukee, St Paul & Pacific, 'F3' 'Pacific', 1910	38	122
Denver & Rio Grande Western, Class 'P-42' 'Pacific', 1913	108	152
Erie, triple-articulated Mallet compound	146	168

	Ref. No.	Page No. Description
Lehigh & New England, 2–8–0 freight, 1911	105	151
Louisville & Nashville, 'K6' class 'Pacific', 1912	39	122
Missouri Pacific, medium-weight 4–8–2 mixed traffic	186	186
New York Central, 'Pacific' type express passenger	184	185
Pennsylvania, 'LIs' 2–8–2 heavy freight	107	151
Reading Lines, high speed 'Pacific' class G–2–SA	40	123
Sante Fé (A.T. & S.F.), 2–10–2 heavy freight	9	110
Santa Fé, 2–6–6–2 Mallet articulated compound	50	127
Southern Pacific, cab-in-front Mallet compound 2–8–8–2	106	151
Texas & Pacific, class 'P1' 'Pacific', 1919	37	121
Western Maryland, class 'H8' 2–8–0 freight	169	178

MAIL VANS AND EQUIPMENT

British
L.N.W.R., lineside postal nets	70	136
L.N.W.R., Travelling Post Office, mail exchange apparatus	73	137
South Eastern & Chatham Railway, post office sorting van	84	141

German
Prussian State Railways, bogie corridor van	72	136

Swiss
Federal Railways, six-wheeled mail van	71	136

RAILCARS

Rhymney Railway (South Wales), steam rail motor coach	23	116
Taff Vale Railway, steam rail motor coach	26	118

SIGNALS

British: Great Eastern, signal gantry at Stratford	181	184
French railways: some typical mechanical signals	27–30	118
Indian: Ouhd & Rohilkund Railway, signals at Cawnpore bridge	114	154
U.S.A.: lower quadrant semaphores	31	119
U.S.A.: upper quadrant semaphores	32	119
U.S.A.: manual block working, double-arm train order signal	113	154

SIGNAL BOXES

Brazil: Central Railways, elevated signal box and signal bridge, Rio de Janeiro	182	184

SNOW CLEARING EQUIPMENT

British: North Eastern, locomotive-propelled snowplough	53	129
Swiss: Bernina Electric, rotary steam snowplough	54	129
U.S.A.: Denver, North Western & Pacific, rotary snowplough	51	128

	Ref. No.	Page No. Description

TUNNEL FAÇADES

British

Bangor tunnel, Chester & Holyhead, western portal	131	161
Box tunnel, Great Western, eastern portal	130	161
Morley tunnel, L.N.W.R., western portal	132	162
Severn tunnel, Great Western, west end	58	131
Shakespeare's Cliff tunnel, S.E. & C., east end	57	130
Watford tunnel, L.N.W.R., south portal	55	130
Watford New tunnel, L.N.W.R., south portal	56	130

Swiss

Lötschberg tunnel, Bern–Lötschberg–Simplon, north façade	129	161

WAGONS

British

Great Central, 25-ton well wagon	12	112
Great Central, 30-ton all-steel bogie coal wagon	122	158
Great Northern, 40-ton bogie well wagon carrying locomotive	78	139
Great Northern, 20-ton 8-wheeled goods brake van	79	139
Great Northern, 35-ton open bogie wagon for bricks	80	140
Great Western, 4-wheel, high-capacity grain wagon	11	111
Great Western, 30-ton bogie covered van	123	158
London & North Western, local mineral train brake van	121	157
London & North Western, cattle-box for working on passenger trains	124	158
North Eastern, 40-ton bogie coal wagon	13	112
North Eastern, high-capacity bogie covered wagon	14	112

French

Northern Railway, U.S.A.-built 4-wheeled box-cars	164	176